# A Guide to Feeding Cats

## A Collection of Historical Articles on Feline Nutrition

By

Various Authors

**British Library Cataloguing-in-Publication Data**
A catalogue record for this book is available from
the British Library

# Contents

A Practical Cat Book for Amateurs and Professionals.
Ida M Mellen..............................................................*page* 1

Care, Feeding and Training of Cats in the Modern Manner - A
Handbook for Cat Owners. Doris Bryant.........................*page* 15

Cat Breeding and General Management. P M Soderberg......*page* 25

Cats. Eleanor Booth Simmons..........................................*page* 31

Cats and All About Them.
L H Fairchild and Helen G Fairchild................................*page* 37

How to Live with a Cat. Margaret Cooper Gay..................*page* 52

Questioned Answered About Cats. Grace Cox-Ife..............*page* 77

The Basic Book of the Cat. William H A Carr....................*page* 84

The Cat - A Guide to the Classification and Varieties of Cats and a
Short Treatise Upon Their Care, Diseases and Treatments.
Rush Shippen Huidekoper................................................*page* 100

The Cat - Its Points: And Management in Health and Disease.
Frank Townend Barton.................................................*page* 104

The Cat Manual. Dick Whittington..................................*page* 109

The Complete Book of Home Pet Care. Leon F Whitney.....*page* 114

The Complete Book of the Cat. Milo G Denlinger..............*page* 120

The Pet Book. Anna Botsford Comstock.........................*page* 123

Tibs Cat Book - A Reliable Guide to the Proper Care and Feeding
of Cats and Their Treatment During Illness; Including Notes on
the History and Evolution of Cats Through the Ages.
Tibs............................................................................*page* 125

# THE FOOD OF THE CAT

"Asparagus and cream and fish
Are objects of his Freudian wish."
—CHRISTOPHER MORLEY

## NATURAL AND ARTIFICIAL FOODS

To LEARN how to feed an animal we ask, "What are its natural foods?" The cat is an omnivorous animal which, in a natural state, subsists on birds, rodents and other small land animals, fishes and other water creatures, snakes, insects—and vegetation. Under domestication this fare has been greatly augmented to include shellfish, ham, roast water fowl, beef, lamb, fruits, garden truck, the milk of cows and goats and other dairy products, bread, cake, ice cream, etc.

The cat's love for milk is not greater than that of many other animals and also birds that never have it in the natural state. Even a parrot loves milk. Miss Viola Irene Cooper of New York City informs us that "Polly loves milk better than anything else; she will get a regular talking jag on after a few plentiful sips." All the big cats of the zoos love milk. Formerly milk was considered injurious to high-bred animals, and when Mrs. Clifford B. Harmon, twenty years ago, maintained her twenty-five thousand dollar cattery at Greenwich, Connecticut, the inmates received no milk, but one-half pound of meat a day, together with oats and olive oil. Some cats refuse milk, some dislike catnip, and an occasional cat will eat no meat. The tastes of the animal under domestication still are changing, and individual tastes differ as among human beings. It is wise to try out one's cat and learn what it likes best.

Eating grasshoppers makes a cat thin; liver should be fed sparingly; with raw rodents dangerous parasites are ingested; and, as it will be seen that the natural foods are largely acid-forming, too much alkalization is deemed inadvisable. Doctor Leon Roth of New York City says that starches may safely form only one-fourth of the diet—corn more than twenty-four hours from the stalk, winter squash, macaroni, peas, beans, potatoes, etc.

*Vitamin A* is needed for growth, weight and eyes. It stimulates night vision, helps prevent kidney and bladder stones, and aids reproduction and longevity. In the natural state the cat gets Vitamin A in fish, the livers and eggs of fishes, frogs and other small animals, and in grass. Under domestication it gets it in milk and other dairy products, oysters, mutton fat, cod or halibut liver oil, vegetables and legumes, and orange juice.

*Vitamin B* is required for appetite and nerves. In the natural state the cat gets it in fish roe, in the liver, kidney and brains of fishes, rodents and birds, and in fresh greens and grass. In the home it gets it in milk, whole wheat bread, yeast, barley, nuts, cereals and many vegetables such as white potatoes, cabbage, raw carrots, peas and parsnips.

*Vitamin D* is good for teeth and bone growth and to prevent rickets. In nature the cat gets this vitamin in frogs and snails, in bird and rodent livers, in the eggs of various small creatures such as fishes; and in the home it is served in dairy products, bread, liver and cod or halibut liver oil. Everywhere the cat gets it in the sunshine it loves so well.

Many people never give their cats any starchy foods, but most cats are very fond of white potatoes, and some that have lived for more than twenty years ate them all their lives. Most cats love corn, even off the cob; some love onions and will play and caper with an onion and then eat it with the tears rolling down their cheeks; nearly all cats love garlic to such an extent that odorless garlic was prepared for them before it was marketed for the human table; some love beets, lemon peel, melons and coconut.[1] Some cats prefer mushrooms to meat, and they all love noodles, particularly when cooked with chicken, also meat and cheese sandwiches. One cat helped himself to a cucumber in preference to a lamb chop which was lying beside it, one ate frog's spawn, and another liked earthworms, while one Persian cat's preference was for grapes, figs, dates and cucumbers. Others have been fond of tea, coffee and beer. Wood's celebrated cat, Pret, would leave even fish for meat prepared with cayenne pepper, and he loved bottled stout. Some cats love mustard, though the phrase "As a cat loves mustard" is satirical.[2]

A cat, out of fondness for a person, will nibble from his fingers food which it would not touch otherwise.

Some cats cannot take fresh milk but can digest diluted canned milk; and evaporated milk diluted 50 per cent with water or barley water is better

[1]One cat, Laddie, owned by the Misses Ida Huyck and Leila Thompson of Oneida, New York, is so crazy for pancakes that he hangs on Miss Thompson's skirt when she is making them until he receives some.

[2]Miss Bowne's cat, Aloysius, of Floral Park, likes fish and beans, asparagus, the juice of black olives, and ice cream if flavored with vanilla, but dislikes gravy. Mickey, owned by Doctor and Mrs. W. M. Rendell of Brooklyn, New York, loves avocados with mayonnaise. Miss Linda M. French tells us that her Catiline would never touch his milk unless he had something more solid first, even if it were only a piece of cold potato.

for them than fresh milk, except in the case of nursing mothers. Some cats cannot stomach canned salmon, and in fact many cats have lost their lives on account of it; yet some have lived to a great age when salmon was the main item on their bill of fare.[3]

We all remember Lafcadio Hearn's kitten "with wings instead of ears," which had twenty-two items on its bill of fare, ranging from beefsteak to tumble bugs.

Many cats go fishing and will enter fresh or salt water to capture their prey. Mr. Edwin H. Perkins of Baltimore, Maryland, a commercial fish breeder, expects his cats to catch their own fish; and we have seen a farmer amusing himself at the end of the day by fishing for suckers, which he placed in a shallow pan from which his cat swished them out with her paw and ate them.

In the tropics, we are informed by Mrs. Beatrice Greig, cats thrive on the same foods as in the Orient—fish and rice, supplemented with vegetables such as eggplant and peas cooked in coconut oil, crackers soaked until soft and then mixed with fish,

---

[3]Miss Sarah Hurd of Oneida, New York, owned a gray-and-white tiger cat named Bunty, who would eat no meat but loved vegetables, particularly string beans. He brought bugs and toads into the house and caught mice, but never was known to eat them. This interesting cat lived to be ten years old, and died of pneumonia.

and also, if imported Persians or Siamese, milk. They receive three meals a day. The coconut oil keeps them in good health, but if they seem off color they are given a teaspoon of olive oil.

Some cats belonging to Mrs. Charlotte A. Barbour of New York City will not touch canned fish but like to chew on dry prepared cat foods, and she finds it easy to provide for them by buying enough of one kind of meat or fish to last for several days, cooking it just enough to prevent spoiling, and serving each kind twice a day while it lasts, mixed with cat food or lettuce. Occasional treats of liver are given.

The cat should have two good meals a day, but occasional individuals need three feedings, and the extra meal may be a light one, bread and milk, egg and milk, oyster soup, puppy biscuit soaked in warm water until soft, prepared cat food, etc.

A little malted milk with the whole milk increases the number of its calories and nutritive value. Chunks of raw meat approximate the natural food and are an important feature on the cat's bill of fare.

When the larder is low, as sometimes happens in the best regulated families, odds and ends of things the cat likes can be mixed. Most cats are exceedingly fond of raisins, cheese and nuts, and these foods have the same value as meat. Raisins are rich

*Photograph by Dr. J. B. Pastor*

*Left*: A catnip lover collects his own. *Right*: Male kitten five months old, bred by the author in a feeding experiment in which bread and milk, vegetables, ripine? wheat, eggs, butter and raisins formed a generous fourth of the diet.

*Photograph by Ida M. Mellen*

*Photograph by Walter L. Hamilton*

*Photograph by Walter L. Hamilton*

*Above:* Milk, though not a natural food, is loved by most members of the cat tribe.
*Left:* Many cats eat corn, even off the cob. *Right:* Bunty, owned by
Miss Sarah Hurd of Oneida, New York, never ate meat.

8

in iron, lime, phosphorus, potassium and other minerals, and excellent for both cat and kitten. If the cat needs building up, merely a change of diet for a few days will help. A fast day now and then, say once a month, is beneficial to the internal machinery of all but very old cats that have decreased their intake.

The well-fed cat not only is a better mouser, but keeps himself in finer condition, the flow of saliva being weakened by absence of sufficient food.

A cat can be trained to eat at the table, and its manners are charming.

## STANDARD CAT FOODS AND DRINKS

*Drinks:*

Water

Milk in any form (goat's milk, evaporated and condensed milks should be diluted 50 per cent with water or barley water)

Tomato juice (occasionally)

Fruit juices

Broth of meats and fish (including canned oyster soup)

*Soft Foods:*

Barley

Cereals cooked and raw, especially wheat

Custard

Bread and rice puddings

Junket

Raisins

Bread

Eggs, cheese, butter[4]
Fish pudding[5]

*Fruits and Vegetables:*
>   Any, raw or cooked, that the cat will accept. (This includes peas and beans.)

*Salt:*
>   A little salt is required with the food.

*Bone-meal:*
>   May be sprinkled on the food.

*Fish and Shellfish:*
>   Any fish with bones removed, cooked. (Raw if small and freshly caught.)
>   Any shellfish cooked or raw

*Grass* or a substitute:
>   Celery, lettuce, greens. Oats, barley, canary seed or grass seed may be sown indoors in winter.

*Meat and Fowl:*
>   (One-half pound a day, or three-fourths meat and one-fourth vegetables)
>   Beef, lamb and mutton
>   Rabbit
>   Suet
>   Ham
>   Tripe stewed or raw,[6] also other
>   Raw viscera such as liver and kidney (liver once in ten days)
>   Veal
>   Any fowl (no small bones)

[4]Butterfat is the most nourishing of all known foods and will keep a cat in the pink of condition.

[5]Fish pudding is best made by boiling fresh boneless fish with barley or brown rice, or the liquid may be thickened with bread, puppy biscuit, or a reliable cat food. Or it can be made as for the table.

[6]In England, tripe for cats is stewed in milk.

# THE FOOD OF THE CAT

Horseflesh of guaranteed quality is used in England
*Prepared Cat Foods* of high grade

## THE CAT'S TASTE FOR BIRDS, RODENTS AND FISH

The cat's taste for birds and rodents resembles our own. It shares with us a love for chicken and rabbit.

It must be remembered that the cat originally was tamed by races who looked upon birds as their natural meat and who highly valued the cat's assistance in catching them, and that even in this country cats formerly were trained in linnet hunting to save the California fruit crops.

A cat that is contented with its home does not take up with life in the woods, but many are compelled to return to the feral state because of neglect or ill-treatment, and in the woods they necessarily feast on birds and rodents. The help these cats are forced to give the "sportsmen" in depleting the number of our song birds is deplored by all nature lovers. Hundreds are shot every year by game wardens, and also by "sportsmen" who regard them as rivals.

Cats can be taught not to molest rodents or birds, and they become very friendly with rabbits, rats and mice, also with chickens, pigeons, cage birds and others. As with teaching tricks, however, nothing can be accomplished by blows.

Gos de Voogt, in 1907, pointed out that a queen of England who kept birds and refused to allow cats in the palace denied herself much pleasure, for all she needed to know was that if she took a bird in her hand and made it peck the cat's nose, it would never try to catch one. This method was employed in the case of a kitten introduced as a mouser into the Bird House at the New York Zoological Park. Since becoming a cat she has produced 54 kittens, all of which she has taught to respect the birds.[7] It is said that the same end can be accomplished with a dead bird.

We have already mentioned the value of teaching the kitten the meaning of the word "No." A cat belonging to Mrs. Elizabeth Becker of Ossining, New York, is a case in point. He had very early learned the meaning of "No." When a baby pigeon fell from the nest and was hurt, it was put in a chicken coop and grew very lively and fearless, but could not fly. It escaped from the coop just as Thomas Tiptail came along, and the cat prepared for a catch but was himself caught by the nape of the neck, held up before the pigeon and told "No!" A little later he was stretched out in the sunshine and the pigeon was walking on his back. He had learned that pigeons were the

[7]New York Zoological Society's *Bulletin,* July–August, 1937.

same as chickens and treated them all with respect, but only the young ones took liberties with him.[8]

A cat can be tethered like a dog, with a harness attached to a line with a pulley, but care must be taken to keep it away from trees and posts. A check can be put on the line to accomplish this. Keeping the cat in at night and not allowing it out in the morning until it has had a hearty breakfast diminishes the temptation to feast on birds.

Dogs kill a large number of birds, particularly fledglings, but commonly are trained to let them alone. A cat can be taught in the same manner. The owners of a chick-killing dog were about to kill the animal when they decided to give a fiery old hen a chance to teach him to amend his ways. The chicks were taken out of the coop, the fox terrier introduced. The hen set upon the dog with beak, claws and wings, and a great commotion followed, until the yelping canine broke out of the coop and escaped to the woods. He never touched a chick again. The owners of the dog used the old hen method with equal success in teaching their chick-killing cat to respect the chicks.[9]

The cat also shares our love for fish and does not understand why we value goldfishes and not

[8]This cat was a powerful animal weighing twenty-four pounds, and afterward protected the chicken coop from a fox, which he attacked and drove away.

[9]*The Rural New-Yorker,* January 1, 1938.

minnows. It therefore helps itself to the golden carp in our garden pool. A clever New Zealand horticulturist, Miss Eleanore A. Beagley of Wellington, arranged a false beach of flexible wire around her garden pool which presents the appearance of a firm beach on which a cat may safely set its foot, but actually the netting gives way a little and pussy gets his paw wet sufficiently to withdraw it. The netting then goes back into position, inviting a second attempt, with the same dampening result. This flexible netting barrier has been successful in conserving the goldfishes.

Wrong feeding and overfeeding are the causes of most of the ills which befall cats.

Special feeding of breeding cats, very young kittens, and of invalids is discussed elsewhere in this book.

The feeding of pet cats—neutered males and spayed females—is simple. They do not require much variety. The object is to keep them trim and graceful with a diet not too stimulating for apartment cats; this promotes good health. A fat cat is not beautiful, is apt to be cross, and has little resistance against disease. An overfed cat is inactive.

The amount given at a feeding must be decided by the owner of each cat. A cat should be neither fat nor pathetically thin. A tiny, nervous, active cat sometimes eats more than a large and placid cat. The average normal cat receives two meals daily; he is usually fed the first thing in the morning and at the dinner hour in the evening.

A cat must be kept interested in his food *not* by seeking new things to tempt him, but by feeding sensible food in amounts small enough to insure his being always ready for the next meal. A normal, healthy cat takes a normal and healthy interest in wholesome and sensible food. A cat should not be screaming while his food is being prepared; this means he is too hungry or his diet is wrong and not supplying his needs; or it means he is a noisy and unpleasant cat.

Many foods popularly given cats have little nourishment, and many lack elements necessary for a cat's well-being.

A normal kitten of three months is given three meals daily and all the milk he wants, provided that much milk is not too laxative. He is permitted longer to eat his meals because he may rush off to play before he has really finished. The first thing in the morning, late afternoon, and bedtime are suitable and convenient feeding hours for kittens. If a kitten has a good romp in the evening and a meal just before he is put to bed, he will probably sleep all night and disturb no one.

A kitten cuts his second teeth between four and seven months of age; some are upset by teething and some are not. Usually they require soft food, but if a kitten seems to crave something hard to chew, some large lumps of Kibbled food will not hurt him. If a kitten refuses to eat, have a look at his teeth before assuming he is ill; possibly there is a tooth hanging loose which you can help him get out.

The age at which a cat changes from three to two meals a day must be at the discretion of the owner. Usually it is some time between six and twelve months of age, although some frail cats with dainty appetites have three meals all their lives. A very active, growing kitten eats a large amount of food and remains quite thin; his requirements are really greater than those of a grown spayed or neutered cat. A cat can be cut to two meals when he becomes fat or inactive, or rather, just before that happens.

Regularity in hours of feeding is advisable, but not absolutely essential in the case of grown, healthy cats. The owner of a well-cared-for cat need not rush home just to give the cat his dinner. The cat may just as well be fed at a later hour, provided suitable food is available then. A *too* well-cared-for cat may miss a meal entirely now and then with beneficial results.

The idea that cats know what is good for them is a fallacy. Cats have been known to eat olives, nuts, doughnuts, elastic bands, cigarettes, cigarette ashes, coffee, and chewing gum. It is quite likely that a craving for abnormal things indicates a deficiency in the cat's diet and a veterinarian should be consulted regarding a corrective diet.

Foods which have no particular food value and which cats like too well, such as shrimps, tinned salmon, and liver, may well be avoided. Cats hold out for them and get so they will eat nothing else. The fact that some cats are fed exclusively on any one of the foods just mentioned does not indicate the food is suitable or that the cats are perfectly well or will remain so. Having nothing else to do, they can to some extent sleep off the ill effects of wrong feeding. But of what use either to themselves or their owners are cats that sleep all the time?

Sometimes nervousness and a twitching skin are the first manifestations of improper feeding. Rough, uneven coat, bare patches, ears completely bare of fur, and eczema result from the exclusive feeding of tinned food, from too much starchy food, and from overfeeding of too rich foods.

Almost invariably a wrongly fed cat has a strong and offensive odor about his body and his sanitary pan. This is also true of a sick cat. A healthy, properly fed altered cat has no odor about his body or his pan.

A properly fed cat is eager for each meal and eats with relish. His coat is glossy, his body slim and active, his breath sweet.

Proper and sensible feeding is economical; it cuts down the cost of food and avoids veterinary bills.

*What to feed.* Beef is generally considered the best and most essential food for cats and should form the foundation of all diets. Milk is a natural food for cats. Beef is constipating; milk is laxative; it is possible to feed a cat on just these two things, and keep him regular. Over a long period of time cats have been found to become bored with just beef and milk, unless kept extremely thin and hungry.

As a supplementary food to use with beef, a good dry prepared cat food is economical, gives excellent results, keeps a cat regular and holds a cat's interest in his food. Such a food cuts down the richness and stimulating effect of beef and provides a balanced diet.

Vegetables are not an important nor a natural food for cats. However, many cats like them, and seem better satisfied with their food when some vegetable is mixed with their beef once or twice a week. The prepared cat food should be omitted from the meals when vegetables are given. Vegetables suitable for cats are the non-starchy varieties such as spinach, string beans, asparagus, celery, lettuce—those that grow above the ground. These should all be fresh and they should be cooked.

Vegetables are usually laxative. They have not been found satisfactory for kittens under five or six months of age.

Most cats like broth. It should be made at home; particularly for invalids and kittens, all fat should be removed. Prepared cat food made in broth instead of water is a nice in-between meal for kittens.

Fish is an excellent food for healthy cats. Sick cats, convalescents, and kittens under five months should not have fish. Heavy, oily varieties should be avoided. Fresh codfish is most desirable; boil, and do not over-cook; to make sure there are no bones, it should be gone through twice. Fish so frequently disagrees with cats when mixed with other foods that a safe rule is to feed it always alone.

Eggs are suitable food for cats; raw or lightly cooked, they may be used instead of beef. They are definitely a building-up food; the average cat should not have them too often, preferably in winter.

Lean, cooked meat or fowl left over from the family table may be minced, and mixed with the prepared cat food to make a meal for a cat. If these are fed without the cat food, the cat may like them too well and hold out for them; besides, they are more suitable when mixed with the cat food. A wholesome diet promotes a wholesome appetite.

Titbits and treats should be given only after the regular meal, and not too frequently. Many cats like cheese.

*Catnip.* Catnip is a tonic herb, attractive to most cats; they may have all they want.

If cats tear and chew their catnip toys, it is usually an indication they are starved for catnip.

If kittens pay no attention to catnip it is because they are young; they probably will like it as they grow older.

Cats deprived of catnip for a long period will over-indulge when first it is given them; they will get excited or even intoxicated. Cats accustomed to a little every day seldom get excited and seldom eat much at one time. They really enjoy rolling in it as much as eating it.

In handling breeding stock it should be remembered that catnip is an aphrodisiac.

*Feeding rules.* Keep fresh water where a cat can get to it at all times. Change once or twice daily, thoroughly cleansing the bowl each time.

Feeding dishes must be clean and sanitary. If the same size dish is always used it is quite easy to estimate the amount of food without weighing.

Food must be room temperature or warmer; *icy cold food should never be given.*

Two or more cats may sometimes eat from one dish; usually it is advisable to feed in separate dishes, and some cats do better when fed in separate cages or rooms.

Thirty minutes is quite long enough to leave food down; what is uneaten should be thrown out. Unless the cat is sick or overfed, or protesting at the introduction of some new food, there will be no food left, and it will be eaten in five minutes. If a cat refuses his regular food, there must be a reason. Don't give anything else. Just omit the meal, watch him closely, and try to determine the cause. It may be that he is overfed, or he may not be feeling well; in either case, no food at all is advisable. The next meal must be given only if he is anxious for it, and it must be smaller than usual, or he may not retain it.

If a cat eats too fast, spread his food over a large plate.

Wipe up every trace of food a cat may have spilled on the floor around his dish. These food particles attract insects, and they will do the cat no good if he eats them hours later when the food has spoiled.

*Food must be absolutely fresh.* With the cat's sensitive stomach and tendency to gastritis, nothing is so important as fresh food. Special attention must be paid to the purchasing of the cat's beef. Hamburger is dangerous because it may have tainted meat in it, because it is usually too fat, and because ground raw beef should be fed immediately after grinding. Even selecting the meat and having the butcher grind it is dangerous, as what first comes from the grinder may have been standing there several hours.

Unless you are fortunate enough to live near a market that carries bull meat for dogs and cats, top round is about the most economical cut, as there is little waste. Wash the meat before grinding and cut away gristle, discolored parts, and most of the fat. Whether or not any fat is included would depend upon the time of year and the condition of the cat.

Ground beef is best for cats; if it is fed in chunks or pieces, cats do not and cannot chew it properly; sometimes they vomit the chunks; frequently improperly chewed beef causes diarrhea. Ground beef is more easily digested and better assimilated; grinding beef makes it possible to mix it thoroughly with other foods. It would be far better to give beef in one large chunk than cut in pieces, for then the cat would have to chew, thus stimulating the flow of saliva and furnishing the teeth some beneficial exercise.

If the beef purchased is very fresh and in one large piece, several meals of raw meat can be served, cutting off just enough for each meal, grinding, and feeding immediately. Daily inspection of beef soon makes one expert regarding its freshness and at estimating just how many meals of raw meat can be fed before the remainder of the beef is boiled, ground, and set aside on the ice. The feeding of cooked beef is so quick and easy that it is compensation for the extra trouble taken in preparing the raw beef meals. Cooked beef seems just as good for cats as raw beef; in the case of invalids, it is better. Cooked meat keeps well and it doesn't require much planning to have it available for the cats on Sundays and holidays.

Vegetables must be put through the grinder or finely minced; otherwise, they will be neither properly chewed nor properly digested.

If dry prepared cat food is fed in conjunction with beef, it is prepared by pouring the correct amount for the feeding into a pan of boiling water, and letting it boil until the water is absorbed. The food should be fluffy and palatable. It is important to select a good quality food which contains no splintered bones and which is not heavy and thick when prepared in water.

As the meat is always cold and the cat food hot from the stove, mixing them together gives a meal of about the right temperature. The proportion of prepared food to beef varies with the individual cat; the prepared food should not form more than half the diet, rather less. It gives bulk and is fed in sufficient quantity to insure a daily, well-formed bowel movement.

*Suggested feeding schedule for altered cats.* Feed two meals daily. For each meal boil a heaping teaspoonful of prepared cat food in water, and mix with about one and one-half ounces of beef. Add two or three pieces of Kibbled food for the teeth. If a cat is not overfed, he will accept a dish of milk daily. Put milk down regularly, night and morning, until you discover at which time the cat prefers it. A little cream may be added to the milk. For variety, fresh codfish may be given once a week, and vegetables may be substituted for cat food once or twice a week. (Some people feed beef one meal and cat food the other—instead of mixing them.) In extremely hot weather feed even more lightly, but give no cold food.

*What not to feed.* Never feed starchy food, such as potatoes, rice, corn, beets, pastry, and white bread; never feed raw vegetables; avoid strong seasoning. Don't economize by buying beef head or lungs; these will give your cats worms.

*Strong white teeth.* Since cats' teeth have no daily brushing and since most of their food is soft, how are teeth to be kept strong, white, and in good condition? It is very difficult to be entirely successful in this matter, but there are certain things which help. To begin with, if a cat was fed calcium through the seventh month, and his mother was also fed calcium, he started life with sound teeth. To keep these teeth in condition some hard food is necessary. Every firm manufacturing a dry prepared cat food also manufactures a Kibbled food, which is in quite large pieces and very hard. This is safe for cats; bones are not. Never give a cat bones from the table.

*Making a change in diet.* Do not conclude because a cat refuses something once that that is final. At a different time he may like it very much. Also do not conclude that a certain food does not agree with a cat if he vomits it the first time it is given to him; he may simply have eaten it too fast, or he may not have been feeling well that day.

It is quite possible to make a change in the diet of a cat no matter how spoiled he is or how set he may be in his ways. Attempting to starve a cat into eating something is useless, as he loses all urge to eat after he has fasted for several days. The starving must be gradual.

To the food a cat likes and is accustomed to, add very small amounts of the desired food; gradually increase the amount of one, while decreasing the amount of the other. Keep him hungry with smaller and smaller meals; a keen edge to his appetite will induce him to accept what is given him.

This procedure may safely be followed with normal, healthy cats; overfed cats should profit by it. Delicate cats, with dainty appetites, usually require a tonic to improve their general condition and stimulate their appetites before they can be disciplined in the matter of food.

Even if a cat will accept an abrupt change in diet, it is wiser to make the change gradual.

No great change is advocated in the diet of a pet cat of eight or ten years of age, provided he has done well on the diet to which he has been accustomed. If, however, such a cat has been overfed, it should be possible to add many years to his life by a change to light feeding.

*Fussy eaters.* There are a few delicate cats with dainty appetites that actually have to be coaxed and pampered. In the majority of cases a fussy eater is just a spoiled and overfed cat.

## Feeding

Probably there is no subject connected with the breeding and rearing of cats which produces more controversy than the subject of feeding. One well-known breeder will be convinced that milk is an essential part of a sound diet, while another, who is equally successful, will assure the purchaser of a kitten that milk should be avoided at all costs as it is the source of most fatal kitten ailments.

The novice is thus presented with what appears to be a flat contradiction on the subject of milk, and the more he reads on the subject of feeding in general, the greater will his confusion become, for milk is by no means the only article of diet over which there is a wide divergence of opinion. Actually, however, the matter is not as difficult as it sounds, for the cat is a most accommodating creature in the matter of food.

When a breeder states categorically that milk is dangerous to cats, this statement really means that he has found that from his own experience trouble has resulted from its use, and it is only natural that he should avoid any article of diet producing unhappy consequences. Quite probably, if milk were again used at a later date in very small quantities, and then gradually increased, there would be no ill effects. A golden rule in the feeding of all livestock is to make sure that new articles of diet are always introduced in the smallest quantities and mixed with food which one has learned from experience suits the animal well.

It is unwise to generalize on the subject of feeding, for cats are very similar to humans in their ability to digest certain foods, and their inability to assimilate others. Some cats thrive on a diet which contains a large proportion of milky foods, while others are always " loose " when milk is fed to them in any quantity, however small. Other cats thrive on a diet which is made up almost entirely of meat, when no milk is ever given.

When a cat or kitten is purchased it is most important to follow closely the diet prescribed by the breeder from whom the purchase has been made, but it would be most unwise to regard this as the only satisfactory method of feeding cats. When the animal has settled down in its new home experiment can begin, and if all changes are gradual the animal can be accustomed to the diet which one considers to be both satisfactory and at the same time the most convenient to provide.

A most important point to remember in the feeding of animals is that meals must be given at regular times. Where feeding is haphazard, and meals are given just when one happens to remember them, condition is soon lost. One must work out a timetable convenient to oneself and then adhere to it. Successful rearing cannot be achieved in any other way.

From the age of ten weeks, when weaning has been completed, until about six or seven months, a kitten needs four meals a day, and a suitable timetable for these meals is, 7, 12, 5, 10.

The first meal of the day may be of a milky nature such as a cereal mixed with milk—some kittens like Oatrex, others prefer a breakfast cereal such as Force mixed with milk. Quite probably one will find it convenient to alternate these foods, and sometimes even to give milk alone. In this matter experience is the only safe guide. Most cereal foods are inclined to be laxative, but this tendency can be checked if arrowroot is added to any milky foods given. It is also a good plan to omit sugar from these milk meals.

The midday meal is one of the main meals of the day and will consist of meat and vegetables which will naturally vary from day to day.

The quantity given at this meal will be gradually increased as the kitten grows, for the needs of a ten-week kitten are much less than when it is six months old. Food is required not only to maintain bodily strength, but for the first twelve months at least rapid growth has also to be aided by increased feeding.

At ten weeks a heaped tablespoonful may be sufficient, but this quantity should be increased to as much as $2\frac{1}{2}$ oz. when the animal is six months old. Males require more than females, as their body size is larger, and usually their rate of growth is more rapid.

WHEN IS THE NEXT MEAL?

Kittens, if healthy, have very keen appetites, and approach their food with a zest which needs a certain amount of control. They always seem to be afraid that they will lose part of their meal if they do not eat it in record time. Bearing this fact in mind each kitten should have its own separate dish at each meal.

When a kitten is ravenous for its food one should carefully consider whether this is just the nature of the cat, or whether it is that management is at fault, or that there is some other reason to account for excessive hunger.

Although far more harm is done to kittens by overfeeding than by the reverse, one should certainly see what effect is produced by increasing the size of the meal, and if, after this is done, appetite is still keen but not ravenous, a solution will have been found. When, however, one is convinced that the size of the meal is adequate, and yet the kitten is always hungry, even between the normal feeding times, and in spite of this appetite does not put on a lot of flesh, one should then suspect worms.

Some kittens are just greedy, and most Siamese are notorious offenders in this respect.

It is a good plan to remain with a kitten while it is eating its midday meal, for one can then check it if the meal is being eaten too quickly. By taking the saucer away from time to time there will be an opportunity for some food to reach the stomach while the œsophagus empties itself. When kittens " wolf " their food one of two misfortunes usually happens. Either the animal suffers from flatulence for a considerable period or the whole meal is returned as soon as it has been eaten. When the latter alternative takes place, the animal should be allowed to rest for a short while, and then a small meal can be fed by hand, a piece at a time.

There is no need to be disturbed because a kitten does not masticate its food, for that is not necessary for sound digestion in cats. Provided that the food has been bitten into pieces small enough to be swallowed, the entire process of digestion takes place in the stomach and intestines.

It is quite a good plan to give a meat meal sometimes consisting of pieces so large that they cannot be swallowed. A solid lump of meat cannot be bolted, and the animal is bound to bite it. This provides excellent exercise for the jaws, and ensures also that a reasonable time is taken over the eating.

It has been suggested that the food given to kittens should all be passed through a mincer, and that the size of the cutters used should be regulated according to the age of the kitten.

There is apparently only one advantage in preparing the food in this way, and that is that it will prevent the animal from picking out what it likes, and leaving what it should also eat but does not find appetizing. Cats as a whole, however, do not appreciate a meal which is presented in this form. It is far better to give them something which they can swallow, and if appetite is naturally keen they will also eat those items of the meal which are not so palatable to them.

The remaining two meals of the day should in make-up be similar to those already described, although the evening meal will be more appreciated if it is not a mere repetition of that given at midday. Variety does much to whet appetite, and a dull, monotonous sequence, even of favourite foods, will soon blunt the edge of the keenest hunger.

No food should be given between meals, and no titbits from the table should be allowed. Many kittens like bread and butter, and jam and cake, but would keep in far better condition if they never learned these little parlour tricks. A human being has some right to ruin his digestion if he wishes, but there is not the slightest justification for teaching a cat to become equally self-destructive.

### Feeding Dishes

Considerable care should be shown in the choice and care of the dishes used for feeding, as an unsatisfactory receptacle for food or milk may produce unhappy consequences.

Some fanciers believe in the use of enamel dishes, and these have much to recommend them provided that they are discarded as soon as the enamel becomes chipped. With care such dishes should last a long time, but sooner or later pieces of enamel will be broken off, and the metal beneath will rust and may become a breeding ground for bacteria unless the dish is carefully washed with boiling water after each meal.

In the average household cups are broken more often than saucers, with the result that there are usually many saucers in excess of the daily needs. These will make satisfactory feeding dishes for the cats, with the great advantage that china is easily washed and disinfected. Even with saucers, however, one should discard them when they are chipped, and this, under normal conditions, is not expensive.

China and enamel are the only materials which can be safely used, and plain metal and wood should always be avoided. Scrupulous cleanliness in the matter of feeding is one of the essentials for successful kitten rearing, and neglect to wash the dishes regularly after each meal is carelessness which tempts providence.

It is far easier to kill kittens by neglect than it is to rear them.

# The Right Feeding of Cats

ADVOCATES OF RIGHT FEEDING
for cats are sometimes confronted by this difficulty,
that some cats, like some people, appear to thrive on
food that has hardly any proper nutriment at all. Just
as a debutante will put in a strenuous day of social
engagements on a breakfast of orange juice and
a luncheon of black coffee and cigarettes, so you find
apparently healthy cats who eat nothing but liver,
or salmon, or bread and milk, or something else
that is lacking in the food qualities that an animal of
the feline race requires.

But if you follow these peculiar eaters long enough,
you generally find that there is a day of reckoning.
I once met a woman who had purchased a handsome
Persian male cat. She believed that meat gave cats
worms, also fits, and she boasted that she had
worked out for her pet a perfect ration, consisting of a raw fishcake, a spoonful of baked beans,
and a soda cracker, all mixed together into a paste.
This was the cat's dinner, and he never had any-

thing else. He was a year old and seemed in great form. But a year later I saw the woman again and heard that her cat was dead. Some disease had attacked him, and he seemed to have no resistance.

A liver-fed cat may seem all right in fair weather, but it is the beef-fed cat that can resist disease. I have always believed in beef because, long ago, two beloved Persian blues of mine who had started life under a sad handicap (their mother died during an operation when they were born and at first they too were thought to be dead) lived, on a diet of the best round steak twice a day, to the great ages of fourteen and seventeen years.

Nature is the great guide. All feline creatures in a wild state are carnivorous, and you cannot do better than to feed your cat as the big cats in the woods and jungles eat, with the modifications that a confined life calls for. Wild cats run so much that they do not need much roughage in their food, and the little demanded is supplied by the feathers and other stuff they swallow with their game and the grass that they nibble when their stomachs ask for it. Our pets, living in the house, eating trimmed meat, must have more bulk in their diet, so we must mix vegetables with their meat, and provide pots of growing grass for them. It is said that cats require a certain nutritional property that exists in feathers. A good way to supply this is to give your pet an occasional raw chicken head with the feathers left on.

Breeders do differ considerably in their methods of feeding cats. The Champions, mother and daughters, who came to America from England a score of years ago, and whose Persian silvers were famous, were strong for meat and not very much else. In a manual published by Dorothy Bevill Champion, entitled *Everybody's Cat Book*, she wrote, "Cats should be fed strictly on a meat diet; no oatmeal, no rice, no potatoes, and no milk. Milk is a cause of dysentery, and no milk-fed cat is free from worms."

But an English contemporary of the Champions, also successful as a breeder, gave her cats a varied diet including bread and milk; liver, boiled and raw; soaked dog biscuit; raw meat and breakfast oats stewed together; fish with boiled rice, turnips, carrots, parsnips, beans, and peas; and occasional meals of prepared cats' food.

Fanciers, raising cats on a large scale, are in a position to experiment. But it is safer for individual owners of pet cats to stick to a simple diet, and if you accustom your cat from the beginning to eat sensible things you will have little trouble.

From the age of three months, two meals a day—breakfast in the morning and dinner at night—are enough, with a drink of milk at noon (fresh milk or evaporated milk thinned with water, as the cat prefers). Remember that your cat is like yourself: it likes its meals warm and appetizing, and slightly salted to bring out the flavor. Never leave food standing around when it has finished eating, and do not feed at odd hours.

Fastidious cats dislike chopped beef from the butcher's, and there is always a chance that it is not fresh. Buy good beef and cut it up, with scissors or a sharp knife, into fine pieces or long thin strips. Some cats like it raw, and some like it slightly broiled. For a change give broiled, roasted, or stewed lamb, mutton, chicken, any kind of fish that is not too rich, stewed rabbit, and almost any kind of game, but no pork, no fried food, and no fishbones, chicken bones, or chop bones. A plate of chicken bones may seem a great treat for your cat, but they have a bad way of splintering and getting lodged in the throat or the intestines.

With the meat at dinner mix some non-starchy vegetable—spinach, asparagus, string beans, or carrots. For breakfast the meat may be supplemented by brown bread toast, either crumbled and mixed with the meat, or broken up in milk. Nibbling a slice of hard toast is excellent exercise for a cat's teeth, and usually is enjoyed if the toast is buttered. Cereals are all right if they do not prove too laxative, but only as an accompaniment, not a substitute for meat.

Once a week, but not oftener, give a meal of raw liver. Olive oil, a teaspoonful once a day, is good for some cats, and they will take it readily mixed with flaked sardines. With some cats, however, it does not agree. If there is a tendency to constipation, add a teaspoonful of agar (a tasteless substance sold by druggists) to each meal. Bran can be used instead, but agar is less harsh. Remember that milk is not a substitute for water. Your cat's special belongings should include a water dish, and it must be washed and dried once a day and kept filled with fresh cool water. Most cats are thirsty little creatures.

The amount of food a cat needs must be determined, more or less, by the owner. Individuals differ. Of course there are rules, such as the orange test mentioned near the close of Chapter IV. Dr. Hamilton Kirk, the noted English veterinary, author of a standard book on *The Diseases of the Cat*, thinks that the daily average for grown cats should be half an ounce of food for each pound of body weight, and that three quarters of this should be meat. But some cats are more active than others and need more food, some are greedy and want too much, some are finicky and must be coaxed to eat. Watch your pet, therefore, and gauge its meals by its condition.

Cats that have acquired a stubborn taste for wrong foods are a problem. Sometimes you can cure them by letting them go hungry for a time, but I have known cats that would starve rather than give in. Diplomacy works better, if you can take the trouble. I once cured a sardine addict by mixing beef with sardines in increasing quantities until, in a few weeks, she was eating beef with only an occasional sardine on the side.

There are many prepared cat foods on the market. but to my mind their sole virtue is that they save owners some trouble. Advertisements tell us that the products contain everything that a cat needs, but nothing out of a can or a box equals good fresh meat and vegetables. At the Ellin Prince Speyer Hospital for Animals in New York, where about thirty thousand dogs and cats are received annually, only fresh foods are purchased, and this is the case with most breeders I know. One objection to canned foods is that some of them contain horse meat, and nowadays few horses are sent to the slaughterhouse except those that are old and diseased. Dry foods in boxes are safer, but too constipating for the average cat.

Above all, never give any prepared dog food to a cat. The stomachs of the two animals are quite different.

# FEEDING

The first thing to remember in feeding the cat correctly is that it is a carnivorous or meat eating animal. While it is capable of adjusting itself to various foods, it needs lean raw meat as the basis of the diet.

We once heard a conversation between a veterinarian and an effervescent woman which amused us and at the same time gave us food for thought. It seems that the woman's pet cat had been very sick with an intestinal upset. After sitting up nights to bring the animal back to health the veterinarian advised the owner about feeding after the cat had returned home. He mentioned meat, fish and eggs. "But, doctor," said the woman, "*I* think Tommy should have vegetables. I give him string beans and carrots and sometimes he even eats raw sweet corn right off the cob." "So," remarked the veterinarian dryly, "and I suppose you feed your saddle horse beef steak?"

Lean raw meat should be fed at least once each day. For kittens the meat should be put through the coarse grinder once. Older cats can be given the meat in larger pieces to encourage chewing. Shoulder beef is good because it is tough enough to develop teeth and keep the gums healthy, and it is also easy to remove its layers of fat. Some breeders prefer horse meat. If it is fresh and can be bought from a reliable dealer it has the advantage of being cheaper than beef and is also tough and lean. All foods should be heated to body temperature before being fed as cats are apt to vomit if food is eaten while too cold. They will not touch it if it is too hot, either.

The other daily meal should consist of fish, dry (farmer style) cottage cheese, liver, heart or kidney. If fresh fish is fed, it should be carefully boned or steamed so that the bones are not sharp and brittle. Canned salmon, mackerel and sardines (canned in water for pets) are excellent cat foods. The sardines are just as healthful as the salmon and are not nearly as expensive. Liver will be relished better if dropped into boiling water and left until it changes color and has cooled before being fed. Dry cottage cheese which should be fed once or twice each week, works wonders for a slightly upset bowel because it changes the bacterial content of the intestine. When your cat catches a mouse, don't take it away. Mice are natural food for cats and give them needed food factors.

To vary a cat's diet feed roast beef, chicken, turkey,

shrimp (as a treat, but not as a steady diet because it is too rich), dry kitty kibble, roast lamb, etc. A beaten raw egg, which may be fed often, is fine to bring out the gloss of the coat. Some breeders with a great many to feed rely on chicken heads once or twice each week to furnish a really natural food. But it is best to remove the feathers and steam the heads in a compression cooker. Mrs. Virginia Cobb who owns the well known Newton Cattery finds cooked fresh tripe useful in her feeding program.

The subject of milk for cats is one for controversy. Some seem to tolerate it very well while others immediately develop very loose bowels and sometimes diarrhea after drinking it. If milk is given at all, it is safest to use diluted canned milk. Fresh or canned goat's milk is readily assimilated by most cats. However, after a kitten has been completely weaned, trouble may be avoided by leaving this item of food off the diet list.

Cats do not readily digest the stringy fibers of beans, carrots or corn and harm may be done the stomach and intestine by giving such foods. Cereals are not a natural food for cats, either, and should be avoided in coarse form. One pet can easily be fed on table scraps if one steers away from fats, starches and fibrous vegetables.

While it is true that the cat as a "feline" cannot under some circumstances digest foods like those mentioned above, it is equally true that the cat as an animal needs all the food factors supplied by nature just as does the human animal. So, to keep them in the best of health, to produce sturdy kittens with bright eyes, sleek coats and good muscle tone they should be given added vitamins each day in the form of codliver or haliver oil, brewers yeast and tomato juice. A pinch of edible bone meal should be added to the kittens' food until they are six months old and past teething age.

Pregnant and nursing queens need the added calcium to help form bone and teeth in their kittens. In catteries where the kittens get their added vitamins on their ground meat from the time they first begin eating solid food they think that is the way meat should taste—seasoned with codliver oil, tomato juice and a crushed brewers yeast tablet. Kittens brought up this way will never present the problem of "How to get the stuff down them?" Most cats, however, like brewers yeast and some will even steal a bottle and work at the lid for hours trying to open it and get to the yeast.

Fresh water should be available at all times. Many people have the mistaken idea that cats do not drink water. Nothing could be further from the truth. A cat will beg for fresh water as pitifully and as plainly as it begs for food.

As every owner knows, a cat likes to chew a blade of grass or two almost every day. The juice seems to provide something he needs. So give him grass, either by allowing him to go into the yard where it is growing, or plant grain seeds (oats, barley or rye) in a flower pot so that he may chew the tender shoots when they sprout.

Some important things to remember well are: Feed at specified times each day. Do not overfeed cats or kittens, and do not leave food before them all the time. When people say that they cannot get their cats to eat as they should it is usually found upon inquiry that the animals have been spoiled by permitting them to eat only one favorite thing to the exclusion of all else, or that they are overfed. It is not a kindness to overfeed. The cat will become lazy, inclined to skin trouble and may even die. An average meal for a grown cat is one-eighth to one-quarter pound of food at each meal depending upon size. A cat or kitten should be eager for his meals. If habitually lethargic toward food, he may have been given too much. If he refuses a meal, pick up the dish and let him wait until the next. If still food is refused the animal may be sick.

Besides the danger of overeating caused by leaving food constantly within reach is the danger of food contamination by flies with consequent risk in the event such food is consumed. An animal is as ready prey to spoiled food as are human beings.

Beginning to eat between three and four weeks of age, the kitten usually helps himself to a few bites of the mother's dinner. The first of such pickings is fish, probably because of the strong odor. A kitten should not be forced to take solid food before it does so voluntarily, though it should be encouraged by regular offers of food at feeding time, and in a very few days will recognize meal time as well as the older cats. At the start the kitten should be allowed about one teaspoonful of food for each meal; if any is left on the dish, allow the mother cat to finish it, or throw it away. Do not spoil babies by leaving food around for if they get hungry, they can always get a snack from the mother's breast. For each kitten's beginning diet the following menu is suggested: .

Breakfast—1 teaspoonful ground, warmed, lean beef
1 drop concentrated codliver oil
¼ brewers yeast tablet

very small pinch of coarse, edible bone meal (the kind used to feed hens)

½ teaspoonful tomato juice

Lunch—1 to 1½ teaspoonsful pablum mixed with one teaspoonful canned milk and enough warm water to make a thin gruel which can be easily lapped up by the kitten. If milk seems to loosen the bowels mix the pablum with water only. Continued loose movements may indicate one of the rare cases in which pablum is to blame. If so, discontinue it and give part of a beaten egg for lunch. Some kittens seem to get along better from the very first on two meals a day, but since their stomachs are so tiny it is reasonable to suppose that more meals and in less quantity would be best.

Supper—Two nights each week give 1 teaspoonful cooked or canned fish, being very careful to crush all bones.

Two nights give 1 teaspoonful cottage cheese.

Two nights feed 1 teaspoonful liver cut fine.

One night feed two or three teaspoonsful of raw, beaten, or soft-boiled egg.

With growth of course, the amount of food is increased. As the mother's breasts begin to dry, the kitten will take less and less nourishment from her and need more solid food. At six weeks he will be taking a heaping tablespoonful of food at each meal instead of the teaspoon he started with. At this age the mother should be taken away from the kittens for several hours at a time during the day and returned to them for awhile only after their solid meals. Their stomachs will be full of food and, while they will nurse as soon as they see her, they will take less and less milk and so help her dry up naturally and pain-lessly.

At eight weeks, after two weeks of gradual weaning, the mother should be removed entirely from her kittens although it is a good idea, if one has wire runs, to keep her in the next cage where she can watch the kittens and so will not fret about them. Morning and evening feedings should now be increased to about one-eighth pound of meat in the morning, one-sixth pound of fish at night and, on the "cottage cheese nights," a large tablespoon of the cheese. Other foods should be given in correspondingly increased amounts. From eight to twelve weeks the kittens are amazingly hungry, grow very fast and are apt to look quite lanky. The added vitamins should be increased gradually along with the increased food until at three months the kitten is getting three drops of concentrated cod-liver oil, one brewers yeast tablet and one or two tea-

Fig. 18
BLUE (Persian) KITTEN
Mar Vista's Don Juan
Bred and Owned by Mrs. Philip C. Jacobs

spoonsful of tomato juice daily. This amount of the added vitamins is correct for cats and kittens from three months of age on.

At three months the kitten may be placed on a two-meal-a-day diet and the pablum and milk discontinued, also he may be fed the same amounts of food as a grown cat—about one-quarter pound of meat, one-fifth pound of fish, etc. At this age one is also safe in branching out with a greater variety of foods. Up to three months however a kitten is a delicate animal and must be fed carefully.

Pregnant and nursing queens should have larger amounts of food. Some breeders provide about one-third more at morning and evening feedings while others prefer to give an extra meal in the middle of the day. Either method is all right, depending upon individual idiosyncrasies. We have some queens which will throw up a meal if it is larger than usual while others can and will eat the increased amount, but refuse an evening meal if they have had something in the middle of the day.

## *Vitamins*

Few cat owners realize the importance of vitamins in the care of their pets. Many times cats are fed on one particular kind of food alone and thus are deprived of essential elements including the vitamins. They may not show the effect of deficiency for some time but eventually it will weaken the cat in some way. Much has been said about vitamins in treatment of human beings. As you well know, most people eat a wide variety of foods, naturally deriving certain vitamins from each. But the cat, if for instance fed on a straight meat diet, will lack almost all of the vitamins and deficiencies of the kind can result seriously.

**Vitamin A.** It is found in pure form in carotene, a yellow plant pigment. It is also present in large amounts in fish liver oils such as cod and halibut. Milk, butter and egg yolks contain the substance. It is also present in fresh green vegetables and some yellow vegetable foods. Not all of these items are particularly suitable for cat food, but for the sake of completeness they are listed here.

This vitamin is necessary for normal structure and function of the skin, mucous membranes, glands, the conjunctiva—(tissue of inner eye-lids and outer side of eye ball) and for normal retinal (eye) function, also for normal growth and development.

**Vitamin B Complex.** A complex group of food factors go together to make the vitamin known as vitamin B. Each one is in itself an important element in the prevention of certain deficiency diseases. The more important ones are listed below:

**Vitamin B₁.** Excellent natural sources of this vitamin are dried yeast and yeast concentrates, whole cereals, pablum, brewer's yeast tablets or powder. It is necessary for normal appetite, digestion and assimilation of food, for normal growth and development, for normal reproduction and lactation in the female. We have seen cats deficient in this vitamin grow so weak in their legs that they could not stand up; the muscles were flabby and the tissues sore. They quickly recovered when fed two tablets of brewer's yeast three times a day. For prevention use one tablet each day. Cats love it and it can be placed on their meat food.

Other effects of deficiency are loss of appetite, impaired digestion and assimilation, malnutrition, retarded growth and lowered levels of general health and resistance.

**Vitamin G (B₂) Riboflavin.** Excellent natural sources are yeast concentrates, liver, milk, eggs and meats. It is necessary for growth, development and maintenance of health. It may also be concerned in maintaining healthy skin.

**Vitamin C.** Ascorbic or Cevitamic Acid found in fruit juices, especially citrus fruits, tomatoes, potatoes and raw vegetables. For the feeding of cats tomato juice is the most valuable source of this vitamin. Mrs. Virginia Cobb of Newton, Massachusetts was the first to suggest a cocktail for kittens which contained a mixture of tomato juice, codliver oil, and calcium. Enjoyed by kittens and grown cats this is an excellent way to give this important food. For cats that do not like this mixture the juice can be mixed with ground beef.

Vitamin C is necessary for normal structure of teeth, bones, bloodvessels and bloodforming organs. Lack of this vitamin results in scurvy, a disease characterized by weakness, anemia, a general undernourished state, swelling of the legs; a spongy condition, sometimes with ulceration of the gums, hemorrhages into the skin and from the mucous membranes. During infection animals need more of this vitamin.

**Vitamin D.** This is perhaps better known to the average person than any of the other vitamins because of its importance in the prevention of rickets. It is often called the "sunshine vitamin" because the ultraviolet rays of the sun or from special lamps activate many oils producing it. Egg yolk and fish liver oils such as cod and halibut are rich sources. It is necessary for healthy structures of bones and teeth and appears to have some effect upon the general health in older cats as well as kittens.

Codliver oil and halibut liver oil is almost indispensable in a large cattery. The straight oil can be given in teaspoonful doses mixed with the meat. The concentrated oils can be given in doses of two or three drops mixed with food each day. One can soon see the effect of the oil on the coat, which takes on a glossy, smooth texture.

### *Pellagra Preventive Vitamin.* Nicotinic Acid.

The importance of this vitamin which is a specific for black tongue in dogs has only recently been discovered. Rich sources are dried yeast, meats, vegetables, eggs and milk. Nicotinic acid protects the digestive tract, skin and nervous system against changes characteristic of pellagra.

**Vitamin E.** This is necessary for normal fertility in experimental animals though its importance in human metabolism has not been determined. Wheat germ oil, lettuce, liver and eggs are all excellent natural sources. If cats seem to need this in order to reproduce it can be obtained in pure form in capsules.

**Vitamin $B_6$.** This is a part of the Vitamin B complex found in rice polishings and yeast. It prevents and cures some of the symptoms of pellagra condition not cured by nicotinic acid, Vitamin $B_1$ or Vitamin G ($B_2$).

# *How to feed a cat*

## TO COOK OR NOT TO COOK

Did you ever see a cat fry a mouse? Then why should you cook for a cat? Cooking, even for the likes of you and me, is a comparatively recent invention. Millions of people living in the world to-day never saw a stove; a sizable percentage of them never even saw a fireplace with a chimney. They cut their meat in chunks, impale the chunks on sticks which they hold over a fire until the meat begins to scorch; then they eat it, burnt on the outside, raw inside.

People cook meat because (a) it keeps longer, and (b) it tastes better. In these days of sanitation, refrigeration, and a butcher shop around the corner, preservation isn't much of a consideration, so most people cook meat to improve the taste. Where other methods improve the taste we still eat our meat raw. To wit: Westphalian ham, Italian prosciutto, chipped beef, and many other sorts of smoked, jerked, and dried meat, sausages, and fish.

Cat's don't think cooked meat tastes better, and they'd rather preserve it inside them.

The notion that raw meat will give cats worms is an old wives' tale. Cats get various kinds of worms from rats, mice, fleas, lice, the grass blades they nibble in the back yard if worm larvæ happen to be roosting on them, and even from their mammas, if mamma has worms. They can get trichinosis from raw pork and a certain sort of tapeworm from raw fish. They cannot get any kind of worms from government inspected beef, lamb, mutton, or veal fit for human consumption, whether it is done or raw.

A lot of people argue that feeding an animal raw meat will "make it vicious". If raw meat would make a cat vicious, cooked meat would too. Meat is simply protein, and the method of preparation cannot possibly affect the eater's disposition.. The only thing that happens when a cat is fed raw meat is that it becomes a healthier, happier, and smarter cat than if it got meat with some of the good cooked out. Maybe you've noticed that the butcher's cat is smart—you didn't think butchers instinctively picked smart cats, did you?


## STEAK OR SPINACH .

There's also the cherished notion that the carnivorousness of cats is a vulgar habit which can be cured by means of a genteel diet of vegetables. Then, when the cat shows signs of malnutrition as a result of this genteel diet, a tonic seems to be the answer. The sort of person who feeds a cat vegetables isn't likely to select a sensible tonic, and the final result usually is a collection of empty bottles and a dead cat. People who disapprove of carnivorousness shouldn't try to live with cats.

The cat has long, sharp fangs to catch and kill its mice and other vermin, and sharp-edged molars to cut them to swallowing size. The cat has no flat-surfaced teeth with which to masticate crispy-crunchy cereals or peanuts or radishes. The strong front teeth which enable men, monkeys, and mice to gnaw raw apples and corn on the cob don't amount to shucks in a cat. If a cat should wish to eat an apple, it would have to bite off chunks with its back teeth—you try it some time!

Vegetarian animals have very long intestines to help them digest their corn and beans. Omnivorous animals have moderately long intestines. The carnivores have exceedingly short intestines, and cat guts are short even for carnivores. Cats' stomachs secrete digestive juices that make the most of any meat that comes their way, while trying to ignore dietary oddities. You can't reform a cat's stomach.

Cats, like all meat-eating creatures, chew grass and nibble an occasional strawberry (foxes do eat grapes, you know). Cats need small quantities of vegetables. House cats in particular need something green three or four times a week. A spoonful at a time is plenty because vegetables serve as a cat's spring tonic, a combination laxative-and-hairball-remover,* occasionally as an emetic. Any vitamins obtained thereby are strictly coincidental and are not to be confused with a piece of meat.

That dab of spinach left from dinner, the string bean Puss swiped while you were stringing them, the three or four peas she batted around the floor, a lettuce leaf and a sprig of parsley will last a cat a week. Or you might

* See discussion of hairballs.

*Watches politely to see if you're going to eat it yourself*

plant grass seed in a flower pot and let Puss graze at will. Cats like growing greens better than grocery store vegetables. They like them so much that it's hard to keep ornamental plants and cats under the same roof unless you keep the plants in the cat, where they're not very ornamental. Cats just love ferns, petunias, nasturtiums, verbenas, marigolds, parsley, besides catnip, of course, and almost anything else a nature-loving person might wish to grow.

Cats are rather choosy about their food. A hungry cat gives you no peace until you feed it; when it has had enough to eat, it quits. I don't know anything more exasperating than trying to coax a cat to finish a perfectly good dab of meat, not enough to save and too much to throw away. The cat listens to your wheedling, watches politely to see if you're going to eat that bite yourself, decides you aren't, scratches all around the dish with the impersonal thoroughness of a street-sweeper, and walks away.

## OVERFEEDING

Of course you can overfeed a cat if you set your mind to it. Choosy as they are, cats can be overfed, underfed and badly fed. They can be, and often are, shockingly misfed by people with the best intentions imaginable.

Overfed cats usually get too much of what is good for them, and get it too often. Most cats know when to quit. Very few cats know when to start. Feed a cat a big meal, give it a few hours to shake down, and the cat will be ready to eat again. A cat on its own catches a mouse, takes a nap and wakes up ready for another mouse, which it probably won't catch; certainly it doesn't find a mouse waiting to be caught every time it wakes up. If you provide the equivalent of half a dozen mice every time the cat feels peckish, you'll soon have a fat, lazy good-for-nothing on your hands.

The person who lives alone with a cat is most likely to overfeed it. First, you give the cat its breakfast, and the last bite of your scrambled egg. Then at lunch time you feel mean and selfish and greedy eating all alone while poor Puss watches every bite and wistfully begrudges it, so you give the cat a little liver pâté, or a speck of cream, or a chop bone that hasn't much meat on it anyway. And come dinner time Puss gets a big meal, with maybe a snack at bed time. I know how you feel, I've felt that way and I've stuffed a cat; but it isn't fair to the cat. The alternatives are to let the cat stare, which will spoil your own meal; lock it in the bathroom; or skip lunch—it probably wouldn't hurt you to skip lunch.

## UNDERFEEDING

There is no excuse for underfeeding a cat. Cats don't ask much and they're pretty tolerant about your choice of food. People who aren't willing to spend a nickel a day on cat food don't want a cat and the sooner they get rid of it the better. Unfortunately, few if any such people will read this book.

## MONOTONY

Monotony is almost as bad as starvation. I met a woman once who fed her cat canned shrimp and nothing else; you never saw a sorrier looking cat. People who feed cats the same thing day after day usually excuse themselves by saying they're not going to pamper a cat, or they haven't time to shop around, or, "It's good cat food, isn't it? Why shouldn't he have it every day?" Those same people complain that they are tired of roast lamb by the time it becomes hash. No one thing is all-satisfying enough to nourish any domestic animal indefinitely. The fact that a cat can drag along for months, or even years, on canned shrimp, or prepared cat food, or even liver, doesn't mean that it is satisfied or well nourished. It isn't.

## FOOD FOR THE WORKING CAT

The worst-fed cats of all, oddly enough, are cats that work for a living. A stupid superstition has grown up in the minds of people who keep cats to catch vermin that a well-fed cat won't hunt. Those people know they can't do a good day's work if they're anæmic, run down and weak, and how they expect a half-starved cat to be successful is beyond me. Common sense should tell them that starvation is weakening, and that weak, slow cats can't catch mice.

Only starving cats will eat rats, and starving cats don't catch many rats. Also, eating rats often makes cats sick and sometimes kills them. A cat that has once been made ill may starve to death rather than eat another rat. Rats are filthy, disease-carrying, dangerous creatures and we shouldn't permit cats to eat them.

Cats do eat mice. But a mouse is a very small animal and it takes a lot of mice to fill a cat. Any cat that has to depend entirely on the mice it catches is likely to go hungry most of the time.

The notion that cats can live on milk and what they

catch is only slightly less crazy than the idea that cats can live on what they catch and no milk.

I don't think cats consider the vermin they catch to be food. I think they regard hunting as a profitable sport, or an enjoyable business—a paying hobby. Some cats are industrious hunters and some are not. Some are efficient mousers and are afraid of rats. Some are killing fools and some specialize.

Starvation will not turn an incompetent cat into a good mouser, and starvation most certainly will ruin a good cat, or any other cat.

## WHAT TO FEED A CAT

Don't think you have to buy filet mignon; the cat would just as lief have shin—liefer, probably. All the cheap cuts of meat, plus the innards which people don't much like anyway, are good cat food. Organic meat is best. A cat that does its own hunting nearly always eats the innards first, leaving the muscle meat for later, if ever. Regardless of breed, all cats eat and need the same food.

### INSIDES

*Liver.* Liver is the traditional cat food. I have known cats that lived to a ripe old age on liver alone. I'm told that years ago butchers used to give liver away to people with cats because nobody would buy it. Now that we know how nourishing liver is, we eat it ourselves and say it is too expensive for the cat. Calf liver is expensive food for anybody, and not a bit more nourishing than any other sort of liver.

Many people consider pork liver unfit food for cats because raw pork can give a cat, or any other creature that eats it, trichinosis. Trichinæ live almost exclusively in the muscles of the pig, and glandular organs such as liver and kidneys are not at all likely to be dangerous. Cooked pork liver, like all cooked pork, is absolutely safe, and pork liver is good cat food for a change.

Cats can adjust themselves to a steady diet of liver if they must. When a cat is unaccustomed to liver its insides are startled when liver suddenly shows up. Liver as an occasional treat has two handicaps: raw liver acts as a laxative; cooked liver constipates. You can turn this to advantage by feeding the cat raw liver to correct constipation, and using cooked liver to check diarrhœa due to sloppy food, such as soups and stews, which aren't good for cats anyway.

*Kidneys.* The cats I live with like kidneys best of any food. They eat beef, lamb, veal, and pork kidneys with equal delight. Unlike liver, kidneys do not startle cats' insides.

*Heart.* Heart is very good cat food, cheap and nourishing. One kind of heart is as good as another.

*Lungs and brains.* Lungs and brains are more nourishing than they look. They look awful. Cut-up lungs look like bloody marshmallows. Brains are pallid and slippery.

Before the war and rationing made peculiar kinds of meat a necessity for cats, I didn't consider such oddities food for anything. Then I discovered that cats had no such prejudice. Ma, Pickle, and Charlie lived on lungs and brains and little else for a long time and stayed in beautiful condition. They were crazy about lungs. They were less crazy about brains.

*Tripe.* Tripe is said to be nourishing. I'm not so sure about that, and anyway cats don't like it. Tripe is listed solely for the record.

## MUSCLE MEAT

While cats prefer innards, I think they thrive best on a diet composed partly of innards and partly of muscle meat.

*Beef.* All cuts of beef are good for cats, though most prefer cheap cuts because they contain less fat than steak and cats hate to bite into fat. A little fat won't hurt a cat, if he likes it, and it won't help either. Fat in any considerable quantity is definitely bad for cats.

I never knew a cat that liked ground meat, even when the meat was lean and the cat hungry. Cats seem to dislike the texture of ground meat. Their no-good little front teeth can't properly bite into it; they get their faces dirty and have a hard time mashing a bite to swallowing size. If hamburger is the only meat you can get, shape it into balls about the size of marbles and maybe the cat will eat them.

*Lamb and mutton.* Lamb and mutton rank next to beef as cat food. Raw lamb or mutton with the fat trimmed off is best. Mutton is so cheap that I wonder more people don't buy it for cats.

Cats have a lovely time with breast of lamb; the bones don't splinter and cats like to chew out all the cartilaginous connective tissue, which is full of good, healthy, bone-building calcium.

*Veal.* Many people believe veal is unfit food for cats. To hear them talk you'd think veal was practically poisonous. That the cow should be the staff of life to cats, and the little calf a menace, doesn't make sense. Belief in the danger of veal originated in pre-refrigerator days when veal was fairly risky food for anyone because it spoiled quickly.

Nowadays veal is as safe as beef or lamb. Cats like it.

*Pork.* Pork is the last meat for cats. Raw pork, no matter how carefully inspected, may contain the larvae of trichinae. Trichinae are worms, microscopic at some stages, which settle between the muscular folds in humans and animals and cause trichinosis. No cure for trichinosis has been developed, and any person or animal that eats raw pork and gets trichinosis is lucky if he lives to regret it. Thorough cooking absolutely destroys trichinae, and pork for any use must be cooked done before it is safe to eat. This includes the innards.

Even though you cook it ever so long, pork, except innards, contains too much fat to be good cat food. Innards are good cat food, when cooked.

Ham and bacon should never be fed to a cat. Smoked, corned, or salted meat may make a cat ill.

### EGGS

If you would have a cat with shining fur, feed it eggs occasionally. An egg is a whole chicken in the making; it contains everything needed to build a healthy animal, and every cat should have an egg or two a week.

Eggs are not day-in, day-out cat food because too many eggs will give a cat diarrhœa.

Raw eggs are best. Some cats won't eat raw eggs, and in that case soft-boiled, poached, or scrambled eggs are all right. Fried eggs are greasy and difficult to digest. Hard-boiled eggs are constipating.

The only thing wrong with eggs is that they don't stick to the ribs. Give a cat two eggs, which ought to hold it until to-morrow, and within two hours that cat will swear by Bubastis that it hasn't eaten for a week. Sensible people ignore such protestations; others, including me, give the cat anything to shut it up. This may be your chance to work off some of that ersatz cat food you got stuck with.

### FISH

Everyone knows that cats like fish. Any sort of fish or crustacean is good for cats, provided it is fresh enough for you to eat. Spoiled fish will kill a cat.

Fish absolutely must be cooked. Fish and pork are the two inviolable exceptions to the rule that you're a sap if you cook for a cat. Tapeworms in one of their complicated larval stages live in fish, and feeding raw fish to a cat simply invites tapeworm.

You must also bone the cat's fish. Cats mustn't have fish bones ever, not big bones or little bones or sort of soft bones or any other kind of bones. A fish bone may stick in the cat's throat and choke it. A swallowed fish bone may puncture the stomach wall. A cat's stomach contains enough hydrochloric acid to dissolve any bone eventually. Unfortunately bones don't wait to be dissolved. If your cat has had fish bones and survived that was pure accident and may not happen again.

For a cat that goes outdoors, fish is fine as often as you are willing to cook and bone it. If the cat can't go out don't feed it fish too often. It is hard to live in an apartment with a cat that has had fish every day for a week; after a while the whole place smells like the Fulton Fish Market at low tide. Fish once in a while will please the cat and won't bother you.

### POULTRY AND GAME

This looks like a pretty fancy heading for a paragraph on cat food. It isn't really. Even city cats can have chicken gizzards and chicken heads. Once in a while rabbits can be bought at cat food prices, and how cats love them!

The butcher will give you chicken heads if you ask, whether you're buying chicken or not. If you can stand the sight of them they make swell cat food. Chicken heads are the exception to giving cats poultry bones; the head bones don't splinter. You give them to the cat just so, no cooking. If you're squeamish about the repulsiveness of chicken heads you needn't even unwrap the parcel, just put it down and run.

On general principles I'd cook rabbit for a cat, though cats are not subject to tularemia, and certainly they don't cook the rabbits they catch.

Poultry bones, except heads, must not be given to cats; they may splinter and become as dangerous as fish bones. If you'd ever seen the misery of a cat with a bone in its throat, or the slow, agonizing death of a cat that had its stomach wall punctured, you wouldn't let any cat friend of yours within a mile of a sharp bone.

### PREPARED FOODS

The prepared foods that come in cans or jars or paper containers may be nourishing but cats don't like them. Those foods are packed in sanitary plants and only Government inspected meat is used, what there is of it. If more meat were used, more cats would eat the stuff. If you should find a prepared food that the cat will eat, consider it an emergency ration, not everyday food. It isn't nourishing enough. Canned fish is fine for a change. Take the bones out.

Some people think dehydrated foods and dog biscuits are suitable cat food. If any cats think so I haven't heard about it. Even Charlie, who likes a very small dog biscuit at teatime, wouldn't consider eating one for dinner, and Charlie's main object in life is stuffing Charlie as full as possible.

Dehydrated foods or crumbled dog biscuits may be used to stretch a kidney and fool a cat if there isn't enough meat to go around. This can be done because the aroma of kidney is extraordinarily pervasive. It isn't nice to fool a cat very often.

There's nothing wrong with these concoctions, you understand; but there isn't enough right with them to interest a cat.

If the packers would set their minds to it and turn out something that cats would eat, the sales would be surprising.

## PÂTÉS DE LA MAISON

Some people simply love to cook for cats and this book won't stop them. One of my best friends cooks for her cats. Mary prepares this recipe in quantity and doles it out as needed to Oscar, Oscar's daughter Mittsy, and her son Rinso. All three are in beautiful condition, so if you're dead set on cooking for cats you might as well have a good recipe:

### Pâté Oscar

1 lb. lung, boiled in very little water.
1 lb. fish, boiled separately, also in very little water, and carefully boned.
2 cups crumbled dog food.
½ cup tomato juice.
1 teaspoon cod liver oil.
Grind the cooked fish and lung together. Pour the liquid the fish was cooked in over the dog food, mix and let cool. Combine the ground lung, fish and dog food, add the tomato juice and cod liver oil. Pack in jars and keep in the refrigerator until used.

This recipe may be varied indefinitely. You could substitute dry toast for the dog biscuit. You could use kidney, liver, heart, shrimp, brains, or chicken gizzards in place of the lungs or fish or both.

## BONES

Cats are not very efficient bone gnawers. Most cats pick at a big bone and leave it. I never knew a cat that didn't love dangerous little bones. Large beef or veal bones are safe because they don't splinter even if the cat bites pieces off. Bones from the breast and neck of lamb are safe. Leg of lamb bones are safe and uninteresting to cats. Lamb chop bones are risky and alluring; cooked chop bones splinter and raw ones may splinter. All other bones are potentially deadly.

## VEGETABLES

Vegetables should be fed to cats in doses, not in portions.

The following vegetables usually agree with cats, and most cats will eat some of them:

Boiled string beans, asparagus, onions, leeks, green peas, carrots. Also grated raw carrots, broccoli, tomatoes, lettuce, celery, parsley, chickory, endive, chives, spinach, corn salad, and mustard greens.

Cats must never have starchy, greasy, or highly seasoned vegetables.

A few cats like fruit, particularly grapes, oranges and berries.

A grown cat should have half a clove of garlic mashed into its food about every two weeks as worm insurance.

## TABLE SCRAPS

Plate scrapings are an inglorious medley at best: fat, bones, congealed grease, gravy, potatoes, and over-seasoned vegetables; everything a cat shouldn't have.

Also, it is practically impossible to feed a cat table scraps and stay friends with your family. Cats don't regard table scraps as food, and consequently they drag bones and fat around the floor like make-believe mice and leave them in strategic places for people to slip on or turn an ankle.

If throwing away table scraps makes you feel wasteful, get some chickens.

### LIQUID REFRESHMENT

Cats must always have access to clean, fresh water.

Some people think that if cats drink milk they don't need water. Others say they never saw a cat drink water, so why put water out for the cat? Cats do drink water. House cats that are deprived of water soon learn to drink from the toilet or the aquarium. Some cats prefer the toilet or the aquarium after a while. It's a bit nicer to give the cat its own water-bowl.

Whether they drink milk or don't drink milk, cats absolutely must have water. Cats need water more than most animals because they wash so assiduously. The fact that cats dislike the clammy feel of wet fur does not mean that they never get thirsty.

Milk is all right for kittens and somewhat overrated as food for adult cats. Some cats are exceedingly fond of milk. Some cats are indifferent to milk. Milk disagrees with some cats. Some cats like milk even though it makes them sick. Some cats don't like milk. Find out which group your cat belongs to and use your judgment.

A cup of milk with an egg beaten into it is nourishing and satisfying, if it agrees with the cat.

Cream makes cats fat and unsightly; you know there's no Charm School for cats.

## TEMPERATURE

When you feed the cat always make sure the food is about room temperature. This is as important as the right kind of food and plenty of water.

If the food is hot, wait until it cools, no matter how the cat clamours. To give a hungry cat hot food is really unkind.

Cold food can kill a cat. If the cat thinks it's starving, you know better, so let Puss wait until the food warms, or you warm it over a pan of hot water.

Cold milk is just as bad as cold meat, worse, maybe, because cats drink faster than they eat. Hundreds of kittens are killed every summer by people who play with them until they're hot and tired, and then pour kitty a nice big bowl of milk right out of the ice box. People kill themselves the same way, but they really haven't any business doing it to kittens.

## HOW MUCH FOOD?

Some cats look like scarecrows on less than half a pound of meat a day. Some cats thrive on next to nothing. Only the cat you live with can tell you how much food it needs to stay in good condition. If a new cat comes your way, take a quarter of a pound of meat a day as the basic ration, and work up or down from there.

A quarter of a pound of lean beef, lamb, mutton, or veal, liver, kidney, or heart will about equal six ounces of brains, lungs, or boneless fish, or two large eggs.

## HOW OFTEN

A grown cat needs one meal a day, not breakfast, lunch, dinner, and a snack in between. Possibly one cat in a million needs breakfast because it doesn't eat enough dinner to keep in good condition; your cat isn't likely to be the millionth one, and I'm not going to tell you how to sin.

I know this is repetitious, but cats simply must not have: raw fish, raw pork, fish bones or fish with the bones left in, poultry bones or any other small bones, ham, bacon, corned beef, sausages, bread, potatoes, cake, pie, spaghetti, macaroni, noodles, baked beans, any other kind of dried beans or peas, fresh lima beans, turnips, parsnips, the cabbage family (including sauerkraut and excepting broccoli), corn, alligator pears, bananas, breakfast foods, porridge, coffee, tea, cocoa, cocktails, candy, popcorn, peanuts, or cheese.

Anything not mentioned in this chapter as suitable cat food, whether listed above or not, should be strictly avoided.

No hot food. No cold food. No highly seasoned food. If you stick to the rules you'll have a healthy cat.

# IF THE CAT WON'T EAT

If the cat refuses food which you consider perfectly good cat food, take the dish away and let the cat wait until to-morrow. Skipping a meal won't hurt a healthy cat. Coaxing a cat to eat is a waste of time. Leaving dishes of uneaten food around won't tempt the cat and will draw roaches.

If the cat refuses food two days in succession and still seems healthy, you're entitled to suspect hairballs or constipation. The treatment is the same for either.*

* See section on hairballs.

If the cat cries for food and then won't eat, the odds are about even that it has (a) a toothache,* or (b) a hankering for something else. Deal with the hankering your own way.

If the cat refuses food and acts sick, you rush it to the vet. Fast.

* See section on toothache.

# How to feed a kitten

A kitten is a baby cat, not a baby cow or a baby horse or a baby human. When a kitten is about three weeks old its first teeth begin to break through the gums, and the kitten is ready for raw meat. Anyone who is shocked at the idea never watched a cat feed kittens. A wise mamma cat starts bringing in mice as soon as her kittens' eyes open, sometimes even sooner, and the moment the kittens have any teeth at all she starts feeding them mice, and teaching them how to catch mice, which makes a mouse a sort of edible primer. A cat that lives in a mouseless apartment will share her own meat with the kittens if they aren't fed properly.

Kittens need exactly the same food as cats, except less

of it and oftener. Don't you believe any sentimental nonsense about how baby kittens are unable to digest meat.

Remember that all cat food must be warmed to room temperature, and this is especially important when you're fixing kitten food.

Remember, cats of any age must always have plenty of fresh clean water.

Some people cut the cat's meat into dainty little bites. Others give their cats hunks to gnaw. Most cats enjoy gnawing hunks. Very young kittens, old cats, cats with toothache and panty-waist cats that are naturally pernickety can't, or won't, manage hunks.

To repeat:

Kittens as well as cats usually dislike the texture of ground beef.

Starches and fats are bad for kittens and cats.

Never feed a kitten or a cat raw fish or raw pork.

Fish for a kitten, as well as for a cat, must be carefully boned.

Poultry bones are absolutely deadly to kitten or cat.

Keep the kitten away from all small bones.

When raising a litter of kittens it is advisable to give each kitten its own dish. This makes it possible to keep an eye on the greedy kitten, and gives the slow one a chance.

Weaning a kitten is dealt with elsewhere.*

The following chart is designed to show you how to feed a kitten from the time it is about six weeks old until at the age of six months it becomes dietetically a cat. In case you don't know how old your kitten is, you can make a pretty good guess by examining its teeth. A kitten six weeks old has a full set of small, sharp teeth. When the

* See chapter: "How to Raise Kittens from Scratch."

kitten is between five and seven months old the milk teeth are replaced by permanent teeth, and the kitten is a cat.

## SIX WEEKS TO THREE MONTHS

### SIX MEALS A DAY

*Breakfast.* 2 tablespoonfuls of milk and egg mixture warmed to room temperature.

To make this you pour the contents of a tall can of *unsweetened* evaporated milk, or a pint of homogenized milk, into a jar, add one slightly beaten egg and shake until thoroughly mixed. Keep this mixture in the refrigerator and warm each portion before feeding it to the kitten.

*Mid-morning.* 1 tablespoonful of lean, raw beef cut fine, not ground,

*or*

1 tablespoonful of raw beef, veal, or lamb kidney cut fine.

*Lunch-time.* 2 tablespoonfuls of milk and egg mixture.

*Tea-time.* 1 tablespoonful of minced raw meat.

*Dinner-time.* 2 tablespoonfuls of milk and egg mixture.

*Bed-time.* 1 tablespoonful of minced raw meat.

Once a week mash half a clove of garlic in the kitten's food to prevent worms. Kittens are more subject to worms* than cats are, and so they should be garlicked oftener. Garlic really does remove ordinary round worms, which commonly attack kittens. It is the only vermifuge which may safely be given to a kitten at home. It won't hurt the kitten if it hasn't got worms. If the kitten smells a bit garlicky for a few hours, that's a small price to pay

* See discussion of worms.

for wormlessness. Besides, you could have spaghetti the same day and then you wouldn't notice. You mash the garlic with a fork or spoon, and wash up as soon as the kitten has eaten, first with cold water, then with hot and soapy. Don't let the thought of garlic scare you—the pyramids were built by garlic eaters. When the symptoms of worms disappear, it is safe to suppose that the worms are gone.

If you adhere faithfully to this schedule your kitten's strength will be as the strength of ten. Scientists have calculated that a hundred and fifty kittens are as strong as a man. I'll bet the scientist who worked that out never raised a kitten, for one healthy kitten can wear out the strongest man in about ten minutes by scampering up and down him, slapping his nose, nibbling his ears, and swinging on his tie.

Be sure the kitten gets meat at bedtime; meat sticks to the ribs best. Also, meat at night won't send the kitten in search of its pan, as the milk mixture will.

Toward the end of this period increase the meat little by little until by the time the kitten is three months old you are feeding it about half as much again.

Always have fresh clean water where the kitten can reach it. (I don't mean to nag—some people don't realize how important it is.)

## THREE TO FOUR MONTHS

### FIVE MEALS A DAY

At three months a kitten is all legs and ears, and you wonder how you ever thought this was going to be a handsome cat. About now a kitten discovers the desirability of washing its face and develops a passionate desire to sharpen its claws on the best furniture. It might catch a mouse.

*Breakfast.* A quarter of a cup of milk and egg mixture, warmed to room temperature, of course.

*Mid-morning.* Two tablespoonfuls of lean, raw beef, lamb, or mutton, or half a lamb kidney.

*Mid-afternoon.* A quarter of a cup of milk and egg.

*Dinner-time.* Two tablespoonfuls of raw meat or cooked fish carefully boned, with a few string beans, or a spoonful of shredded spinach or lettuce. Not more than one teaspoonful of vegetable.

*Bed-time.* Two tablespoonfuls of meat or cooked fish.

Continue half a clove of garlic once a week.

## FOUR TO FIVE MONTHS

### FOUR MEALS A DAY

Now you can vary the kitten's diet by feeding heart, liver, lungs, brains, and kidneys as often as plain beef or lamb. Continue feeding garlic once a week.

Double the quantity of milk and egg mixture in the morning.

Discontinue the mid-afternoon milk feeding.

Move the mid-morning feeding up to lunch-time.

*Breakfast.* A third to a half cup of milk and egg mixture.

*Lunch-time.* Two tablespoonfuls of lean, raw meat or innards.

*Dinner-time.* Four tablespoonfuls of meat or cooked, boned fish mixed with a teaspoonful of any recommended vegetable.

*Bed-time.* Two tablespoonfuls of meat. No vegetables at bed-time.

# FIVE TO SIX MONTHS

### THREE MEALS A DAY

When the kitten is five months old discontinue the bedtime snack, or, if more convenient, discontinue lunch. In either case add that amount of food to the kitten's dinner. Continue feeding garlic once a week.

The kitten should have at least six ounces of solid meat or half a pound of fish or lungs or brains every day, and may need even more. It isn't just sustaining itself, it's making a big cat and burning up energy like mad.

After a kitten is six months old you feed it as if it were a cat. It may not become a cat the day it's six months old, a kitten becomes a cat when it feels like it, but from here on it eats like a cat.

A cat should have one meal a day and milk, if milk agrees with it.

And of course, always, plenty of water.

## FEEDING

**107.—At what age does a kitten start to take food other than its mother's milk ?**

This depends upon the size of the litter and the condition of the mother. A litter of two or three kittens will obtain sufficient nourishment from a healthy mother for the first four weeks. A large litter may need extra food after three weeks.

**108.—What sort of food should the kittens be given ?**

One of the patent dried milk foods is best. There are several made especially for animals and instructions for mixing are printed on the container.

**109.—Why not give ordinary cow's milk ?**

Cow's milk may be given—it should be warmed to blood heat, and a few drops of lime water added to prevent curdling—but kittens usually do better on a more concentrated milk food.

**110.—How often should the kittens have the first milk feeds ?**

Once a day for three or four days, then twice, and so on until they are getting four meals a day.

**111.—Will they lap it from a saucer?**

They should be fed from a small teaspoon for the first few days. After this they will quickly learn to lap if their mouths are gently guided to the milk in the saucer.

**112.—When should they have the first solid food?**

At the age of six to seven weeks.

**113.—Of what should this consist?**

Fresh fish is the most suitable. It should be finely mashed with a little of the liquor in which it is cooked. An alternative to fish is well-cooked rabbit mixed with brown breadcrumbs.

A teaspoonful of finely scraped lean raw beef or mutton may be given instead of either of the above.

**114.—How often should the meat or fish meal be given?**

Once a day up to the age of eight weeks, then two solid meals a day up to nine or ten weeks. The milk meals should be given as well, making up the total of four meals a day. But *never give milk and meat together*—four hours should be allowed between each meal. At eleven or twelve weeks some kittens do better on one milky meal and three solid ones.

**115.—How about the quantity of food given at each meal ?**

In the first stages of weaning a kitten will take about a teaspoonful of food at each meal. This increases rapidly as the kitten grows and by the time it takes its first meal of fish or meat it will be having considerably larger milk meals.

The amount taken will depend on the size of the kitten and the amount of nourishment it is still getting from the mother, but, generally speaking, kittens should be fully weaned by two months of age. They may continue to suck from the mother, but her milk will decrease in value.

A kitten should have as much food as it will take eagerly, but not so much that it causes indigestion or a blown-out appearance. By the time it is six months old, the number of meals can be reduced to three a day.

**116.—Is this method of feeding suitable for all pedigree kittens ?**

I would make a slight difference in the case of Siamese, whose digestions tend to be weak in early life. Many breeders give meat at an early age, but, personally, I prefer fish up to the age of three months. Tinned pink salmon, when obtainable, is ideal, and the soft bones should be crushed and mixed with the flesh.

**117.—Are there other kinds of food that can be given for the sake of variety and convenience ?**

Plenty, once the kitten is really on to solid food, and is thriving. But all changes should be gradual. Any of the following may be introduced into the diet. Chopped cooked carrot or greenstuff, barley porridge, any cereal food, brown bread, cooked tripe, cooked liver, milk pudding, meat gravy, eggs either raw (beaten up) or cooked. Potato should not be given, and any starchy food should be given in small quantities only. These foods may be given from the age of four months onwards.

**118.—What are the signs if the diet is wrong ?**

All or any of the symptoms of indigestion—diarrhœa, sickness, gummy eyes, ravenous appetite and generally poor appearance. See the section dealing with Ailments for further information and treatment.

**119.—How many meals a day should a grown cat have ?**

Two solid meals are sufficient in ordinary cases but a nursing mother needs three. A saucer of milk may be given as an extra meal if the cat likes it. But all cats and kittens should have clean drinking water placed where they can get to it whenever required.

**120.—What quantity should a cat have at each meal ?**

This depends upon the size of the cat and other things. For instance, a cat used at stud needs more food than the household pet. Four to six ounces of meat or fish per day is enough for most cats. Never leave uneaten food about. If the cat does not finish a meal at one sitting give less at a time.

**121.—Is it true that a cat can live on the mice it catches ?**

No, it is not true. The best fed cats make the best mousers. Cats hunt mice for sport, not food.

**122.—Is grass a necessary food for cats ?**

Grass is not a food at all, it is a corrective. Cats eat grass because they are out of sorts. If your cat eats grass it is probably suffering from indigestion caused by incorrect or over feeding.

**123.—Should cats be given bones ?**

Generally speaking, no. Large bones will not hurt them, but cooked rabbit or poultry bones splinter and may cause fatal internal injuries by piercing the intestines. Small bones may stick in a cat's throat. Fish bones should always be removed before the fish is given to the cat except in the case of soft bones such as in tinned salmon or cooked skate.

Cats can get enough exercise for their teeth if meat is given in pieces large enough to be chewed before being swallowed. Many cats are fond of the dry biscuit foods prepared especially for them.

**124.—Some cats seem to like rather odd things to eat, I have heard of cats eating tomato, cake, cheese and so on. Would this be good for them ?**

Yes, if given as occasional titbits. Most cats like cheese and a little finely grated over a biscuit meal will add to its attractions.

**125.—How should biscuit meal be given ?**

Sometimes dry if the cat will eat it this way, but usually it is preferred moist. It should be soaked in no more liquid, either broth or milk, warmed, than it will absorb. Sodden food should never be given.

**126.—Is horseflesh good for cats ?**

Yes, if it is fresh. Most cats like it.

**127.—Should it be given raw or cooked ?**

It does not really matter. But if there is the slightest suspicion of its freshness, it must be cooked.

Some breeders cook all meat, others give it raw. Offal should always be cooked as it may contain the eggs of worms.

**128.—What kind of food would be suitable for a sick cat ?**

It depends on the illness. Cats that are seriously ill usually refuse all food and it is necessary to keep their strength up with liquid nourishment. Glucose dissolved in water, meat juice, milk and lime water, or a few drops of brandy in water are all useful.

If solid food can be assimilated, steamed fresh fish or scraped raw beef alternated with meat jelly or finely minced rabbit may be given. Convalescent cats frequently have capricious appetites and anything likely to appeal should be tried. Do not weary the animal by over persuasion, but try something else later on if the first offer is refused. Sometimes the most unlikely foods will be taken. One cat recovering from a severe attack of distemper refused all offered food but helped himself to some cooked greens from the dinner table. After this he returned to a normal diet. Beaten-up raw egg is a rapid conditioner for cats that have recovered from illness.

# NUTRITION AND FEEDING

$A$ GREAT deal of nonsense is spoken and written about cats, and this is true above all in the area of nutrition and feeding. We are told that all cats love milk; that they should never be fed starch or vegetables; that fat is bad for them; that bones do them no harm.

Perhaps the silliest thing that is said about the cat is that it will, given the opportunity, instinctively choose a balanced and sensible diet.

It won't.

Most cats will choose sugar, white bread, spaghetti sauce, or some other unlikely treat, often preferring such delicacies to fresh red meat.

And yet meat is the basic food of the cat, which is a carnivore. Its natural prey includes many small animals, such as the rabbit, which are herbivorous. In eating these animals, the cat consumes everything: muscle meat, internal organs, the half-digested vegetable contents of the digestive system. In this way the cat's overall nutritional requirements are met.

But the cat that is not feral develops tastes for foods unavailable to cats that have to kill their own game. It is the responsibility of the owner to see to it that the cat gets the proper kind of diet, a balanced diet that will meet all of its needs.

Until recently, that was a difficult task, for comparatively little research had been carried out on the nutritional requirements of the cat, compared with the enormous amount of information available on the dog. In recent years, however, an increasing number of scientists have begun to take an interest in this area of research. The Committee on Animal Nutrition, National Academy of Sciences-National Research Council, has finally brought together the existing knowledge on cat nutrition. This chapter is based largely on that study, prepared by Dr. S. N. Gershoff of the Department of Nutrition, Harvard School of Public Health. This is the first time that this material has been available to the cat owner.*

## PROTEINS, FATS, CARBOHYDRATES

Man requires five major elements in his food: proteins, fats, carbohydrates, minerals, and vitamins. The cat needs all of these with the possible exception of carbohydrates. The need for carbohydrates has not been demonstrated, which does not mean that the need doesn't exist; it just means that we don't know. In case such a need does exist, it may be just as well to provide some in its diet, if the diet is adequate in proteins and fats.

Proteins exist in a number of forms. Each kind of protein is a combination of several of the twenty amino acids. When proteins are taken in through the digestive system, they are broken down again into their constituent amino acids, which are then reassembled in the form of new protein. Surplus amino acids are burned as energy.

Fats are broken down in the body into fatty acids and glycogen. The body then transforms glycogen into glucose, a body fuel. The

* I have also made substantial use of the material on the cat by Drs. Patricia P. Scott, A. Carvalho da Silva, and Marny A. Lloyd-Jacob in *The UFAW Handbook on the Care and Management of Laboratory Animals*, published by the Universities Federation for Animal Welfare of Great Britain, and of research reports appearing in American veterinary journals.

fatty acids are changed into body fats. (Generally the same course is taken by carbohydrates in man, but in a more roundabout way.)

"Most cat nutritionists favor high-fat, high-protein diets for cats," Dr. Gershoff found. "Purified diets containing twenty-five to thirty per cent fat and thirty to forty per cent protein were commonly used. These high-fat rations appear to be more palatable than low-fat diets."

The cat's requirements of proteins and fats are much higher than those of the dog. Over thirty per cent of the diet must be protein, for example, if a kitten is to grow properly; the best results are obtained when the protein content reaches forty per cent.

Cat show exhibitors should be especially interested in one finding reported in England: cats which were "maintained for three months exclusively on lean beef muscle had an extremely good appearance and especially soft fur."

On the other hand, a high-fat diet apparently enables the cat to absorb vitamin A more efficiently than it can with a low-fat intake. "This suggests that many low-fat commercial cat foods may supply inadequate vitamin A," Dr. Gershoff told a conference of veterinarians.

Cats maintained on the high-fat diet were found to accumulate a small amount of fat around the liver, unlike cats fed low-fat diets. Whether the liver fat is harmful has not been determined.

## MINERALS

All animals need minerals—calcium and phosphorus to build teeth and bones; iron, copper, and cobalt to produce healthy blood; other elements for the development and maintenance of all the nerves, muscles, and organs of the body.

The exact amounts of these minerals needed by the cat have not been determined. Until we know otherwise, it must be assumed that the cat needs reasonable quantities of the minerals, in roughly the same proportion, say, as man and the dog.

The effect of mineral deficiencies has been studied. It was found that kittens fed only raw or cooked heart—a diet particularly deficient in calcium and iodine—showed undesirable effects after seven weeks.

These effects included nervousness, inability to coordinate, and finally paralysis of the hind legs. The bones softened and then collapsed, causing the paralysis. The thyroid was affected and so were the kidneys.

When calcium was added to heart in the diet of kittens, the bones did not soften and the thyroid was not affected as it had been. Adding iodine strengthened the thyroid and delayed the weakening of the bones.

A unique problem in considering the cat's mineral needs is the unusual susceptibility of the cat to kidney and bladder stones. There has often been speculation that high-mineral diets might be a factor in this. But several nutritionists were unable to cause urinary stones in kittens even with diets containing as much as thirty per cent minerals.

## VITAMINS

These accessory organic substances are needed for metabolism. They are essential to life and growth. The cat's needs for these vitamins are not necessarily the same as man's.

VITAMIN A: The human body manufactures this vitamin mostly from carotene, but the cat does not, at least not in important quantities. Cats whose diet is deficient in vitamin A lose their appetites and become emaciated. Some show weakness of the hind leg with some signs of stiffness. There are scaly changes in the tissues of several of the organs. The lungs often become inflamed. So do the eyes. The teeth are affected adversely. The hearing and the nervous system are impaired.

Acute deficiencies of vitamin A usually result in death.

Fat in the diet helps the cat to utilize fat-soluble vitamin A, so it is important that there be enough fat in the cat's food.

NIACIN: This is the antipellagra factor in the vitamin B complex. A lack of it in cats results in a feline disease resembling pellagra. The cat suffers diarrhea, emaciation, and death. Often a respiratory disease precedes death. Of forty-five cats used in one experiment, not one lived more than twenty days on a diet without niacin.

FOLIC ACID: Another B complex factor, this vitamin causes

anemia and a sharp drop in white corpuscles when it is absent from the cat's body.

CHOLINE: Also lumped in the B complex, the lack of this vitamin in cats causes weight loss and fatty livers.

THIAMINE (B₁): A cat whose diet provides an insufficient amount of thiamine may suffer from loss of appetite, vomiting, inability to coordinate, abnormal reflexes, convulsions, and heart disorders. One team of researchers found that cats fed raw carp or herring ultimately displayed a thiamine deficiency, but cats fed raw perch, catfish, butterfish, did not.

RIBOFLAVIN (B₂): Cats suffering from the lack of this vitamin lose their appetites, fade away to skin and bones, and finally die. The hair, particularly around the head, sometimes falls out. Cataracts have been observed in chronically deficient cats. Impaired nerve function, digestive disturbance, anemia, sore mouth, poor litters, and poor nursing of kittens have also been reported as results of riboflavin deficiencies.

If the cat's diet is high in carbohydrates, its need for riboflavin is slightly lessened. The reason for this, it appears, is that more riboflavin is manufactured in the cat's intestines when the intake of carbohydrates is high.

PYRIDOXINE (B₆): The deficiency of this vitamin in cats is characterized by stunted growth, emaciation, convulsions (the nervous system is affected), anemia, kidney disease, and deposits of iron in the liver.

ASCORBIC ACID (C): Apparently vitamin C is not required by cats.

VITAMIN D: Rickets, as one might suppose, is the result of a lack of vitamin D in cats, just as in man. For that reason this vitamin, which is essential to the utilization of calcium and phosphorus in forming teeth and bones, is especially needed by the pregnant queen and the growing kitten. The requirement of vitamin D for cats over a year and a half old is believed to be quite low.

VITAMIN E: One effect of an insufficient supply of vitamin E may be steatitis, an extremely painful disease in cats; it can be fatal. (See a discussion of this in the section on commercial cat foods below.)

Vitamin E deficiency also can cause lost litters, sickly kittens, and a drop in the red blood cells.

VITAMIN K: The need of the cat for this vitamin has not been established.

PANTOTHENIC ACID: Loss of weight and fatty livers are among the ill effects that follow upon an inadequate supply of this vitamin.

## CALORIES AND ENERGY

A kitten's caloric requirements are, proportionately, a great deal higher than an adult cat's. The kitten must burn up enormous amounts of energy just producing all the cells that enable it to grow. On top of that, kittens usually play harder than grown-up, sensible cats. It has been noted that a growing cat consumes about eighty calories per pound of body weight every day.

Around the time that kittens are weaned, they need about 125 calories a day per pound of body weight. This drops off as the kitten grows. By the time it is thirty weeks old—about seven or eight months —the kitten needs only about 65 calories per pound of body weight per day.

The adult cat's caloric requirements depend on the kind of life it leads, just as with humans. They also depend on the weather, to some extent, particularly with cats that are permitted out of the house to roam. From the time it is a year old, the cat that goes out for its exercise, chases rabbits, is chased by dogs, and climbs into trees (for firemen to rescue) needs 40 to 45 calories per pound of body weight every day.

Dr. Mark L. Morris, a well-known specialist in animal nutrition, has found that temperature changes have an average effect of about 46 per cent on food consumption. Outdoor cats tend to eat a good deal more heavily at the onset of cold weather in the fall and gain extra weight. However, the food consumption tapers off even though the weather remains cold. The reverse of this process takes place in the spring.

The sedentary cat—and that includes most pet cats, living wholly in apartments or houses, sleeping a considerable portion of the day, playing only briefly, exercising hardly at all—needs substantially fewer calories, in the neighborhood of 30 calories a day per pound of body weight.

A word may be appropriate here regarding obesity. Overweight is less common a problem in cats than in dogs—and far less than in man. The average female cat's weight is between six and ten pounds; the average male's, eight to fifteen. (There are authentic records of cats that have weighed as much as thirty-five pounds!)

Obviously the simplest way to bring down a cat's weight is to cut down its food supply. Unlike its master or mistress, the cat can't sneak fattening treats that aren't on its diet, so a weight-reducing diet almost always is effective. If your cat is sedentary and weighs fifteen pounds, and you want to get its weight down to about ten pounds, figure the number of calories it would require to sustain itself at the ten-pound level, and make that the daily ration. It may also be helpful to add vitamin B complex as a supplement to the diet.

### COOKED OR UNCOOKED?

There are few arguments concerning cat care that can arouse greater passions on the part of some fanciers than the question of whether the cat's food should be cooked or uncooked.

There are some foods, of course, that everyone agrees must be cooked—pork, for one, because the muscle worms that cause trichinosis in man can also kill the cat. And it's generally agreed that fish should be cooked, too. But after that, the arguments begin.

The National Research Council's survey of technical knowledge about cat nutrition examined two studies of the comparative values of cooked and uncooked foods for cats. The survey summarized the reports of these experiments: "Consistently better growth, development, reproduction, and lactation were obtained when raw meat and milk were fed to cats than when they received cooked meat and milk."

Moreover, once the "deficiency state" resulting from the cooked diet "was produced in kittens, it could not be reversed. When deficient adult cats were returned to a raw diet, normal animals were not produced for several generations."

Now, these results must be viewed with a great deal of caution. The diet itself—meat and milk—was something less than ideal. How would those cats have managed on a good canned cat food or dog food? Would vitamin-mineral supplements have had any material effect on the results? Until those questions are answered, it is best to consider this whole matter of cooking like this:

If you are feeding your cat fresh meat, let it be raw. If you are feeding the cat a canned (which means cooked) food or some other precooked food, make sure it meets all the nutritional requirements listed above.

## MEAT

BEEF: Excellent. The best for the cat is muscle meat. Feed it in small chunks or ground. Once a week the muscle meat might be varied with organ meats: "lights" (lungs), heart, tripe, kidneys, or liver. Some veterinarians insist the liver should be cooked.

HORSEMEAT: Good, but fat must be added.

VEAL: Many cats prefer this to beef. Either the muscle meat or the organs will do nicely.

LAMB: It's too expensive to serve your cat the chops, unless you're an unusually generous master, but the kidneys are very good and they are a convenient size for purchasing. Cut up in one-inch cubes, lamb kidney is almost a sure-fire cure of a jaded feline appetite.

PORK: Trimmed of fat, ground, and cooked, pork may make a pleasant change of diet for the cat.

## FISH AND CHICKEN

Fish once a week is a treat and it's good for the cat. It must be cooked, preferably steamed to retain as many of the nutrients as possible. And it must be carefully boned. Even canned fish that's labeled "boneless" sometimes has wicked little spears in it, so be careful.

Shellfish are perfectly acceptable, too, but it's a waste of money—the cat will appreciate mackerel just as much.

Chicken is good for the cat, and most cats love it. (Turkey, too.) Be sure it's cooked, however, and that there are no bones to catch in the cat's throat. One more caution: do *not* let the cat have the skin of the chicken or the turkey. The cat can't digest the skin easily, and it can irritate its digestive system by trying.

## OTHER FOODS

MILK: A great many cats cannot tolerate milk and some of those who can keep it down can't stand the sight of the stuff. One effect that milk has on many cats is cathartic. When milk is given to a cat, it should always be lukewarm.

CHEESE: Occasional servings of cream cheese and cottage cheese are approved by many veterinarians. My own cats love all kinds of cheese, but they don't get them for dinner.

EGGS: Ideally, the cat should get the yolk of a one-minute boiled egg twice a week or more often. It can be mixed with milk or with the cat's other food.

VEGETABLES: Green vegetables, in small quantities, are good for the cat. They can be cooked or raw. If you want to give the cat a treat, get some oat seeds and plant them in a flower box in a sunny corner of the kitchen. The cat will be delighted at the opportunity to eat the green, growing grass. But it won't keep the cat away from your philodendrons, unfortunately.

POTATOES: It has long been an article of faith with many cat lovers that no cat should ever be fed any starch, and particularly potatoes. The theory was that the cat couldn't digest starch. But it can be digested by the cat, provided it is broken in texture before it is ingested. This means the potatoes should be cooked and mashed. Cooked, mashed potatoes were an important part of one of the experimental diets cited by the National Research Council.

WATER: The cat needs water to drink. Some owners who give their cats milk think water is unnecessary. They're wrong—milk is a food, and it's not to be used as a substitute for water. A dish of clean, fresh water should be on the floor, available to the cat, at all times.

## COMMERCIAL CAT FOODS

There is a variety of cat food available in pet shops and super-markets. Today pet foods outsell baby foods in grocery stores through-out the country. Most of this merchandise is of excellent quality—which doesn't necessarily mean it's the best thing for your cat—and is carefully prepared in order to give your cat most of the substances it needs in its diet.

Can you simply open a can of cat food and give it to your pet—and know that it is getting the nutrients it needs? The National Research Council survey answered that question with these words: "Much of the commercial cat food is nutritionally inadequate and must be supplemented with other foods."

It will be noted that *all* commercial cat foods are not lumped in the "inadequate" category, from which fact it can be assumed that some prepared foods are properly nutritious.

This puts the burden on the cat owner to study carefully the labels on available foods. Every label must list ingredients and an analysis of the contents. The ingredients and the analysis should be compared with the requirements listed below.

In general, the cat owner is well advised to alternate a carefully chosen canned food—and don't overlook the dog foods when you're selecting it—with fresh meat.

THE CANNED FISH PROBLEM: An unresolved conflict exists among scientists regarding the dangers of canned fish as the exclusive element in a cat's diet. Until this matter is resolved to everyone's satisfaction, cat owners ought to exercise extreme caution in feeding canned fish to their pets. This is particularly important because several cat foods make a point of advertising that they are all fish.

There have been six reports from research teams that cats fed exclusively or almost exclusively on canned cat food consisting entirely of fish contracted a disease called *steatitis*. In most—but not all—of these cases the fish was red meat tuna. (Because other fish packs were involved, however, the findings ought to be applied to any all-fish cat foods.)

Steatitis is an agonizingly painful disease. The fatty layer just under

# NUTRITION AND FEEDING

## SATISFACTORY LEVELS OF NUTRIENTS
## TO MEET THE NUTRITIONAL REQUIREMENTS
## OF THE GROWING CAT

| NUTRIENT | PER POUND OF DIET[1] |
|---|---|
| Total proteins | 4.6 ounces |
| Minerals | Required |
| Vitamins | |
|   Vitamin A | Required |
|   Vitamin D | Required |
|   Vitamin E (international units) | (34)[2] |
|   Vitamin K | —[3] |
|   Thiamine | 4 milligrams |
|   Riboflavin | (4) |
|   Vitamin B$_6$ | 4 milligrams |
|   Niacin | 40 milligrams |
|   Pantothenic Acid | (5) |
|   Biotin | — |
|   Folic Acid | Not required |
|   Choline | — |
|   Vitamin B$_{12}$ | — |
|   Inositol | — |

[1] The values that are not in parentheses are estimated from various adequate rations, hence are probably in excess of the actual requirement.

The values in parentheses are tentative estimates of the minimal requirement and contain no margins of safety.

[2] Not satisfactory if excessive dietary source of polyunsaturated fatty acids is fed.

[3] Signifies no information is available on a qualitative requirement.

the skin becomes inflamed; the cat displays "exquisite tenderness," as *The Merck Veterinary Manual* puts it, "manifest by resentment" when it is touched on the back or the abdomen. The animal loses its agility; it is reluctant to move at all. The cat becomes feverish and loses its appetite. As the disease progresses, the lightest touch is enough to make the cat cry out with pain. The disease often ends in death.

Why canned all-fish cat food causes steatitis is still not definitely known. When the association of the food with the disease was first observed, it was believed that absence of vitamin E from the diet was responsible. Almost all of the companies packing all-fish cat foods quickly enriched the food with alphatocopherol, one of four forms of vitamin E, and slapped "added vitamin E" labels on the cans.

But a team of researchers at Angell Memorial Animal Hospital at Boston then reported on eight more cases of steatitis traceable to canned all-fish cat food—and four of these had been fed from cans labeled "added vitamin E."

It seemed that the addition of vitamin E was not the answer— at least, not the entire answer—to the problem. Then Danish scientists, studying the same disease in minks, came to the conclusion that "yellow fat," as steatitis is sometimes called, "is primarily due to the contents of marine fat in the feed." They decided that "the most satisfactory method of preventing 'yellow fat' . . . is control of the fat composition in feeds, so that the content of marine fat does not exceed three to four per cent."

The picture is still unclear, for a new report from an American source says that cats in *its* experiments were completely protected against steatitis by the addition of vitamin E to a fish diet.

As an additional complication, Dr. Morris, in his manual on *Nutrition and Diet in Small Animal Medicine,* warns: "The possibility of alphatocopherol containing a toxic factor for cats should be considered. In the preparation of experimental rations for cats, we added excessive amounts of alphatocopherol to the diet. This substance was very unpalatable to cats and the animals would actually starve unless alphatocopherol was removed or added at a much reduced level."

This raises some question as to whether *enough* vitamin E can be added to canned fish to protect the cat consumer.

The only conclusion that can be stated at this time is this: If your cat likes canned all-fish cat food, feed it only such food if it is labeled "added vitamin E." But give the cat this food only once a week. The rest of the time feed it foods that do not include fish.

## SUPPLEMENTS

Everything that has been said in this chapter up to this point should make clear that it is not as simple as it might at first appear to ensure your cat a balanced diet with the proper intake of vitamins and minerals.

This problem becomes more acute when the cat is sick, pregnant, lactating, or growing.

Nevertheless, some authorities believe it is unnecessary to add extra vitamins or minerals to the diet. They meet disagreement from other experts who think vitamin-mineral supplements make good sense.

I'm inclined to agree with the latter group. There is a very slight danger of overdosing the cat, but this is so remote as to be unimportant in our considerations. On the other hand, a vitamin-mineral supplement is a kind of insurance that your cat is getting the proper amount of these two essential kinds of nutrient.

However, it is necessary to be cautious about the vitamin-mineral supplement that is used. One of the supplements most popular with pet owners, for example, provides a seriously inadequate supply of pantothenic acid. The formulas should be compared with the table of nutrients on page 99.

Vitamin-mineral supplements for cats come in many forms: drops, capsules, pills, powders, and small pellets designed to be highly palatable to animals. Supplements intended for use by humans can be used, if you prefer.

## KITTEN FEEDING

The feeding of kittens under the age of five weeks will be discussed in Chapter 9. Here the subject under consideration will be the kitten from weaning to adulthood.

About the time the kitten is five or six weeks old, it can begin to get its first food as a supplement to the milk it obtains nursing. This early food can be a prepared cereal for human babies or a preparation devised especially for kittens. The latter is preferable; it is much higher in protein than pablum for babies (thirty per cent as against fifteen per cent). This is an important point, for kittens grow at a much faster rate than human babies, and so they need a bigger proportion of tissue-building protein. Whichever kind of cereal is used, it should be moistened with warmed milk or with evaporated milk diluted with water.

If the kitten has difficulty taking this food from a spoon at first, stick your finger in the cereal and then let the kitten suck it off your finger as though it were a nipple.

Feed this to the kitten three or four times a day, and let it continue to nurse in between.

After a week or two, it's time for the next step in weaning. Now strained meats of the kind prepared for human babies should be added to the diet. The strained meats should be warmed, of course—everything fed to the kitten should be warmed.

Scraped meats are added to the diet next, then twice-ground lean meat, finally boneless canned fish, finely broken up. The meals can then look something like this:

> MORNING: Warmed milk with a barely cooked egg and baby cereal mixed into it. Vitamin-mineral drops.
> FORENOON: Strained baby meats mixed with baby cereal.
> NOON: Scraped or doubly chopped raw lean meat.
> AFTERNOON: Warmed milk and egg again.
> EVENING: Baby strained meats or doubly chopped raw lean meat.
> NIGHT: Baby strained meats or doubly chopped raw lean meat.

The meals should be cut down to four a day as soon as the kitten begins to show a diminished interest in the frequent feedings. As the baby teeth appear, more solid food can be added: meat softened and cut into tiny cubes, fish carefully boned and mashed, and so on.

In the fourth month, the meals can be reduced to three. After that, two meals a day should be sufficient.

The average kitten weighs slightly more than three ounces at birth. It can be expected to gain about an ounce every three days until it is seven weeks old; it then weighs about twenty ounces. In the next month it will probably gain another ten ounces. The weight will gradually increase month by month—by ten ounces, then by eleven ounces, by twelve ounces, and so on. The top of the growth curve is reached in the ninth month. Then the monthly gain in weight begins to fall off very gradually for the next five months.

# NUTRITION AND FEEDING

## ADULT FEEDING

Many cat owners feed their full-grown pets twice a day. There is nothing wrong in this, but it is unnecessary. Barring unusual conditions, one meal a day is sufficient for almost all cats.

About four to seven ounces of food a day will sustain the average cat very well. In the adult cat the stomach will hold four and a half ounces of food or more. At one feeding the cat can take in quite enough food to keep it comfortably occupied for the next twenty-four hours.

It is well to serve the food in a bowl on the floor—with a generous supply of paper under the dish, for cats love to drag morsels of food out of their dish onto the floor, for no reason that I've ever been able to determine.

The food should be put down for the cat at about the same time every day, for cats are creatures of habit, and essentially conservative. If the cat hasn't eaten its food within a reasonable time—say, half an hour—and shows no interest in it, take it up. *Never leave food down for the cat!* When food is left out for the cat, it attracts insects, dries out so that it is completely unappetizing to the cat, and simply bores the poor cat, who gets sick of the sight of it.

Whether the cat really needs variety in its food is something that nobody really knows. On general principles, it seems no harm to give the cat a change of dish for a day or two now and then.

Sometimes a cat is a fussy eater. Usually this is because it has not been fed in the proper manner in the past—most often because its food has been left down for it all day.

Feeding the cat by hand for a day or two, or petting it while it eats, may induce it to eat properly, especially if its food is set out for it only for a short time each day.

If that doesn't start the cat eating, a meal of diced lamb kidneys will usually stimulate the most listless appetite.

If the cat absolutely refuses to eat anything but food which is not good for it, its food—its proper diet—should be set out for it every day nevertheless. When the cat refuses to eat, the food should be taken up. This should be done until the cat eats. This can be quite a strain on the owner's nerves, for the cat may very well starve itself for a week before surrendering, but surrender it will, in time.

In persistent or recurring cases of inappetence, it is wise to consult your veterinarian. Judicious prescription of vitamins sometimes can help with such problems.

One last word about the feeding of the adult cat: there are several companies which manufacture special formulas of canned cat foods for the feeding of cats with special dietary problems. These foods are available only on prescription from a veterinarian. If he recommends such a food, his advice should be followed carefully.

## SNACKS AND TIDBITS

If a cat has been eating its meals properly, there is no reason why it should be denied snacks from time to time—but only if its appetite for regular meals is good. Little treats, especially prepared to be palatable to cats, are available in pet shops and supermarkets. They are the best tidbits your pet can eat.

Other snacks do no harm. My cats all love cheese, for example, and they're all hearty eaters. So, when I have cheese, they have cheese—tiny little pieces, of course. They also like a little cake, cookies, bread, meat, chili (terrible thing to give a cat!), curried rice (ditto), and so on.

## THE LAST WORD

Remember, above all, that your cat is not the best judge of what he should eat. The National Research Council survey summed it up this way: "Some foods of high acceptability were found to be nutritionally inadequate when used over extended periods."

### DAILY FEEDING SCHEDULE

| AGE | FROM 5 TO 9 WEEKS | FROM 9 WEEKS TO 4 MONTHS | FROM 4 MONTHS TO 1 YEAR | OVER 1 YEAR |
|---|---|---|---|---|
| Number of feedings | 4 | 3 | 2 | 1 or 2 |

# FEED.

In the country, or in a small house where the cat has full freedom of the kitchen and back yard, very little attention is required in regard to feeding, as the animal will pick up from the scraps the very diet which it is best for it to have. When cats, however, are kept in closer confinement, and in city houses, more attention must be paid to their food; for inattention to this is the principal cause of most of the maladies with which they are affected. In the first place, the dishes from which a cat is fed must be absolutely and immaculately clean, and at each fresh feed should be scalded before they are used again. Milk is not only the traditional diet of the cat, but also forms one of the principal articles of food for it. The milk should be perfectly fresh, as sour milk is apt to produce digestive troubles, especially diarrhœa. Sour milk, however, is useful sometimes as an adjunct in the treatment of worms. While the cat drinks a considerable quantity of milk, it prefers water when it is really thirsty, although it takes only a very small quantity of this. The water, like the milk, should be in an absolutely clean pan. There is a very useful pan—which can be found in porcelain at the china-shops, or can be readily made by a tinner—consisting of a pan divided in the center by a partition, in which the milk is placed at one side and the fresh water at the other; this insures that the water is emptied out each time the milk is replaced, in order to clean the pan and allow it to be perfectly fresh. Bread (preferably stale bread) and the ordinary crackers, water biscuit, or oatmeal biscuit, can be added to the milk. Spratt's Patent has a cake for cats which is very useful for occasional diet. Oatmeal porridge forms an excellent diet, and vegetables should be given from time to time. Most cats are very fond of asparagus and celery, but will at times eat almost any vegetable. In cases of diarrhœa or looseness a little boiled rice is a good addition to the milk. There seems to be a prejudice on the part of some people against the feeding of meat to cats, which is unwarranted; and a cat is better for an occasional feed of meat — even once a day in small quantities. They much prefer it raw, and prefer mutton to beef. The traditional cat-meat of the "cat-meat man," which is known so well in England, is made of horse-flesh, and is a wholesome, good food; but the marketing of that is practically unknown in America. Fish is a very favorite diet with the cat, and can be given from time to time; but the fish should be perfectly fresh, as all meat ought to be, for putrid meat is much more apt to produce digestive troubles in cats than it does in the other carnivora; in addition to which, its use by the animal gives it an offensive odor in the house. In résumé, the diet of the cat, with a basis of sweet, fresh milk, can be made up of any of the foregoing articles, if care is only taken to insure the absolute cleanliness of the pans from which the animal is fed, the good condition of the food itself, and that the diet shall be varied. Often when a cat has been kept on one diet steadily for some time it loses its appetite, and appears dumpish, or even ill, when a simple change of food will bring it back to itself at once. Boiled liver is useful once in a week or ten days, or when the cat is a little off its feed, as it acts as a laxative. It is not, however, good diet for regular use.

# FOODS AND FEEDING

IT is customary to feed the house-cat in a very irregular manner, and, through negligence, often not at all : hence the reason why one sees so many half-starved cats about.

The negligence of the average domestic in the matter of feeding house pets is notorious, as these are either fed to excess or overlooked altogether.

The natural diet of the cat is flesh, and such should constitute at least three-fourths of its food ; milk, bread and fish making up the remaining fourth. **Vegetables** are wholly **unsuitable**, and **liver** is too much of a **laxative**, but very suitable as an **occasional** feed, especially during the summer. In London and other cities cooked horseflesh constitutes the principal food for cats, being both cheap and wholesome, either cut up or given whole— preferably the former. If a cat is fed on this, say, for the midday meal, along with a little milk both morning and evening, it is all that it requires.

Another form of flesh is that known as **lights** (that is, the lungs), and cats are largely fed upon this. It is not, however, a good form of flesh, and in some cases constitutes the source of tuberculous infection. Its use should be discouraged at all times.

Table scraps make an excellent article of diet, particularly when meat is mixed with a little gravy and potatoes. Both fresh and salt fish are useful, but it ought to be cooked, although we have seen it stated that salt may actually cause peritonitis— a statement that almost staggers humanity.

Good sound horseflesh and scraps from the butcher are cheap, economical and satisfactory, but fatty substances cats will not take as a rule.

To feed cats upon putrid flesh, fish, etc., is a most pernicious practice, though one, we regret to say, not uncommonly practised.

Kittens, after weaning, should be fed at least four times a day—milk thickened with a little corn-flour, or, what is still much better, " Lactol," the latter being particularly suitable for them.

Directly they are able to take solid food, begin them with fish, say, twice a day.

Small birds and mice, of course, constitute an important item of food whenever a cat has an opportunity of procuring such as its prey, but these cannot always be relied upon as a daily allowance.

Patent cat-foods are sold, the principal one being manufactured by Spratt's Patent, and this is an excellent food, and cats thrive on it.

The author has recommended horseflesh as the best food, but a word of caution is necessary to qualify this recommendation. There are at least two diseases affecting the horse, which might be transmitted to the cat through consuming the semi-cooked flesh of a diseased animal.

Legislation against these diseases is prohibitive, namely, anthrax and glanders. Carcases affected in this manner are not allowed to be cut up, much less distributed as food to other members of the lower creation: the obscurity, however, of these maladies does sometimes lead to their accidental admission into the cat's-meat market, yet this is not sufficient to disturb the recommendation of horseflesh as food for cats.

### Special Feeding of Sick Cats.

When cats have to be fed, artificially, as in many cases of disease, a great deal of trouble and patience has to be exercised, and considerable manipulative dexterity is called for.

First of all, the following artificial foods and stimulants are the principal ones: warmed milk; iced milk; milk and soda water; beef juice; Brand's Essence; Lactol; Oxo; Bovril; raw egg; egg and brandy; corn-flour; arrow-root; malt and beef wine; coco wine; Wincarnis; Liebig's Extract; raw minced meat, etc. For sick cats Lactol is truly excellent.

The main thing to observe in feeding a cat that is ill is to give a **very small quantity**, repeated, say, **six times a day.**

The stomach readily rebels against artificial foods, and if too much is given the stomach is sure to reject it. A dessertspoonful is ample to give each time, and if raw meat is used, a teaspoonful of minced beef-steak is enough at once.

The condition of the patient will be the best guide in regulating the quantity, mode of administration, suitability of the aliment and its repetition. The proper way to give a cat fluids is through a small pewter syringe, which is charged with the material, then inserted at the side of the mouth, and the piston then driven home. Semi-fluids, however, cannot be given in this manner. A teaspoon is commonly used for the latter,—the mouth being held open meanwhile. Even when the greatest care is exercised, cats become very refractory to the artificial administration of either food or medicine, and the remedy may prove more detrimental than the disease, especially if the cat struggles violently meanwhile.

One person should hold the cat by gripping it after the fashion indicated in the chapter on General Management, whilst the second person administers the food. (It is better if a third party is present, to steady the head and to depress the lower jaw, through which a piece of tape may be passed inside the mouth and the free ends then used as a lever, for depressing the lower jaw.) When cats have to be fed by the lower end of the bowel, the chances of recovery are very small indeed. A clyster must be given to clear out the rectum, and the nutrient medium then injected—a little brandy, or brandy and egg, being the best for such purposes.

# FEEDING

There is, in my opinion, only one correct diet for cats and kittens, and that is the natural one—raw meat. A cat living in a wild state lives on birds, mice and young rabbits, and if it was possible to feed show cats in the same way they would thrive amazingly. Such a ménu would be difficult to arrange regularly even in the country, and in a town manifestly impossible, so we must consider the best substitute. Where horseflesh can be obtained fresh and sound it will answer admirably, and is much cheaper than beef or mutton; moreover, in buying horseflesh we can generally get the best steak, whereas in the case of beef or mutton the price charged becomes a serious consideration, and we are obliged to be content with what we can afford. Shin of beef is excellent food for cats, and can generally be bought for about sixpence a pound.

I wish to impress upon cat fanciers that if their cats are fed entirely on raw meat a much smaller quantity of food is required than if farinaceous foods are given, for the latter are not suited to the internal economy of cats, and they require to overload their stomachs before they can obtain the requisite amount of nourishment from them. Raw meat is to the cat a concentrated form of nourishment, and there appears to be little waste when it is the sole article of diet.

Roughly speaking three to four ounces of meat daily is sufficient to keep the largest full grown cat in excellent condition. As a rule cats should be fed once daily, but "bad doers" or invalids may be fed more frequently, and of course only the regular attendant can decide the exact quantity of food to be given to each cat, and the number of meals which it requires. Queens with kittens should be fed twice or three times daily and may be given about two ounces of meat at each meal.

I have found that cats fed in the way I describe suffer from none of the troublesome external and internal complaints of which we hear so much in most catteries. Of course they occasionally catch cold, but they are in such splendid condition that they recover quickly, and even distemper visits them lightly. I never give milk to cats or kittens except medicinally, they have plenty of water to drink, and the little kittens are fed on raw meat before they are a month old. Of course young kittens should be allowed a very small quantity of meat at each meal—about half a teaspoonful twice daily is sufficient for a kitten until it is five weeks old, when the quantity may be gradually increased.

I know that there are many fanciers who will absolutely refuse to believe that a raw meat diet is the best for cats, but I also know that these are people who have not given it a fair trial. I often receive letters from people who say that they have followed my system, but that "of course they gave a little milk food too." This milk food is exactly what I am always preaching against. It does not agree with cats, but causes indigestion and irritation of the lining of the stomach and bowels, chronic diarrhœa and worms. Of course in some particular cases of illness sloppy foods are ordered by veterinary surgeons, but only in very rare cases are they advisable. If a cat suffers from constipation a little milk every morning will act as a mild aperient, and this is surely a proof that it should not be regarded as an ordinary article of diet. When I receive complaints as to the costliness of a meat diet where a large cattery is kept, my reply invariably is " Reduce the number of cats and feed them properly."

# Cats and Their Food

*T*HERE are unknown millions of cats in the world today. In every age since the beginning of history, cats have shared man's food and shelter. And yet, in spite of all the opportunity there has been to observe and study the nature and habits of cats down through the centuries since ancient Egypt, we still know surprisingly little about them. The cat still walks by himself in a kind of mysterious and self-sufficient aloofness.

In the past too many of us, including cat owners, assumed there was little that could be learned about the cat. A cat was "just a cat"—one of those living, semi-automatic creations of nature which was put out at night and occasionally rewarded with a saucer of milk for catching a mouse. We settled back complacently and summed up the little we knew about cats in a few well-worn and contradictory adages: "A cat has nine lives," but "Nothing can be sicker than a sick cat." It is only in comparatively recent years that we have begun to replace these faulty casual observations with reliable scientific information.

There are several types of house cats, distinguished principally by the way they live. By studying each of these groups we have been able to collect a great deal of information useful to the pet owner.

Everyone knows that many cats living a domesticated life have become feral—gone wild. Not everyone realizes, however, that in a wild state cats thrive exceptionally well for the most part.

Actually there are two kinds of *wild* house cats. In one class belong the creatures which have fled human habitations and gone to live as wild animals in the wilderness. They are the ascetics of the cat family. They often fail to leave descendants, and their ranks must constantly be augmented by new converts to their cult. It is known that they frequently live to be quite old. Students of wild life, particularly game wardens who have captured large numbers of feral cats thought to be killing game birds, generally find that these wild animals are in excellent health and condition, a fact which attests to their rugged constitutions and unusual adaptability.

The second kind of wild cat is the rounder—more often a male—who goes from alley to alley in the city and from barn to barn in the country. He is a typical tramp—a scroungy, slinky, mangy, battle-scarred creature who has to elude dogs, dodge stones thrown by rascally boys, and live in spite of the putrescent food and rat poison he finds in garbage cans. He is an entirely different animal from the cat-gone-wild that stalks its prey in the woods. He is hardly admirable, yet one must at least respect his one outstanding characteristic—adaptability.

The comparison between the two wild classes demonstrates one thing clearly: that cats thrive best when they are quite well separated from other cats. The woods cat has less opportunity to contract diseases, virus, bacterial or parasitic, feeds on a diet composed principally of rodents, is less subject to accidents and violence.

Socially there are two general classes of well-*domesticated* cats: those kept for some useful purpose in barns or warehouses, where they save millions of dollars and prevent disease by holding the rodent population in check; and those kept as pets, some of which incidentally kill mice but whose primary purpose is companionship or even ornamentation. In the aggregate, pet cats probably outnumber all the rest.

Owners of the useful type seldom place any emotional value on them. To them a cat may be a wonderful ratter, but neighbors always have plenty of cats to give away or they may be had by the bushel from the Humane Society. What difference does it make if one or two die or disappear? I once made a call on a farmer who had fourteen sleek cats in his barn. When I called again two weeks later there was only one old tom left; all the rest had been wiped out by a disease. The farmer didn't care. The cats to him were not much more valuable than so many turnips; he'd get more as soon as he thought there was no infection left in the barn.

From all these four classes we can learn lessons, but the most useful ones come from those which live *without* the "loving care" of a mistress or master. Obviously we cannot duplicate the conditions under which the wild cats live. Some owners have to keep many cats together in a barn; others like to take their cats to shows; nearly everybody likes to put the cat out to exercise and relieve itself; and many people must board cats at vacation time. In short, we can't always isolate them. Nor can we provide a natural diet of rodents—and we wouldn't want to if we could. Imagine a city owner taking weekly trips to the country to trap field mice! What we can do is to provide food and attention which will keep our pet cats in top condition all the year round. Anything we can learn from observing wild cats or tame ones will help us to do it.

## FEEDING

Many people, including some so-called experts, apparently feel that great variety is necessary in a cat's diet. They sometimes go to astonishing extremes, and if you were to follow their advice you would spend a good part of every day in obtaining, preparing, and storing the cat's daily rations. Fortunately most of their recommendations are based on personal opinion and preference and not on a scientific study of nutritional needs.

The fact that an elaborate diet is unnecessary to cats can be seen by studying the food of the feral cat, who thrives—and indeed stays in beautiful condition—by eating very few types of food. Several accurate studies have been made of the contents of the stomachs of wild cats trapped or shot by wardens. Some of the studies were made, incidentally, to determine the amount of damage done by cats to bird life, and the results seemed to indicate conclusively that cats destroyed far fewer birds than had been supposed.

One of the studies, which dealt with wild cats taken in Wisconsin, found that the contents of the stomachs were composed principally of remains of rodents, birds, and insects. The fifty stomachs examined contained fifty-nine rodents, nine birds, and five insects. A few of the cats had eaten garbage, and in their stomachs were found potatoes, string beans, apple, boiled rice, and custard pudding. Two had eaten ensilage.

In Oklahoma a study of the stomachs of eighty-four wild cats taken from several groups showed that 55 per cent contained mammals, mostly rodents; 26.5 per cent contained garbage; 12.5 per cent contained insects; and 4 per cent contained the remains of birds. In a small group of cats caught in residential districts 6.5 per cent showed evidence of having eaten birds. Other studies have shown that as much as 25 per cent of the contents of cats' stomachs was insects. Lizards also were found in some.

Our principal interest in these lists is not so much in the small number of items in the diet. More important is the fact that these studies all showed that whatever animal the cat fed on was eaten in its entirety. Very seldom do cats open their prey and eat only a single part of the animal, such as the liver or kidneys. Even bobcats—living chiefly on rabbits, hares, squirrels, mink, muskrats, mice, grouse, pheasant, bluejays, grass, insects —eat most of the body of their prey. Red and gray fox fur and meat has been found in their stomachs, and occasionally porcupine remains or venison. But who ever heard of a wild house cat eating only kidneys or liver of a mouse?

Cats do have some variety in their diet, but that variety is largely the result of their eating the complete animal. Rodents eat great quantities of vegetable matter, and when the cats eat the rodents they get a certain amount of this type of material contained in the stomachs and intestines of these animals. In all probability a cat could live indefinitely in excellent health on a diet consisting exclusively of mice. That single item would provide ample variety—muscles, bones, liver, intestines, brain, glands, *and* vegetable material in its digestive tract.

What was said in Chapter 3 about spoiling an animal by unconsciously training it to demand one particular type of food applies especially to cats. The number of cats which refuse all food but one kind of canned cat food, or kidneys, or liver, or halibut, or codfish, or horse meat, or lean beef, is myriad. The problem should be handled just as it is with other animals. It is best to pay no attention to a pet cat's likes and dislikes. Get her hungry enough to eat what is good for her and then see that she obtains in her daily meal the dietary essentials which can be obtained only through variety. But see that the variety is the same as that she obtains when she eats a mouse—variety in one meal. There is no harm, of course, in giving her tidbits as a *small* part of her diet.

Are there any foods which must be excluded? Is it true what some authors say about never feeding starches to cats? Must all their food be cooked? Must all pork be eliminated from their diets? And fat? Folklore notwithstanding, cats can digest starch. Science says they can, and very well, too, if the starch granules are cracked by cooking. How can authors logically condemn the feeding of starchy food and yet advise feeding kibbled food which may be 75 per cent baked starch? Yet they often do. Nor must *all* the food of cats be cooked. They digest raw meat as admirably as cooked meat. Fish *should* be cooked, since if it is fed raw in large amounts, it may cause paralysis. But canned fish has been cooked and is readily available in all food stores. If there is any meat which cats like less than another and tend to regurgitate more often, it is pork. But that is only because pork is a very fat meat. When fat and protein are fed alone, the cat's system does not tolerate it so well as when fat and carbohydrate are fed. If very fat beef is fed, the result is the same. People who advise against feeding pork or fat beef forget that if plenty of carbohydrate is fed along with either or both, the fat will be handled nicely and may safely be fed in reasonable amounts. They forget, too, that when a cat eats a mouse she may get as much as 30 per cent fat—but in that case there is sufficient carbohydrate to burn it up.

What should a cat be fed? There is no "best" diet. Here are several, any one of which is perfectly adequate. The decision should be made on the basis of convenience.

What you yourself eat, so well diced, mashed, or ground together that the cat can't pick out part and leave the rest. Cats will eat all items of human diet when trained to do so. They have even been known to eat olives.

Good canned cat food.

Two thirds dehydrated meal-type dog food, plus one third canned fish or cooked diced meal. Some of the larger catteries feed dog meal and mackerel with sufficient water or milk to produce a moist consistency, thinner than crumbly.

Fish—always cooked—mixed with bread, table scraps, et cetera.

Meat—beef, lamb, pork, horse—mixed with vegetable products.

Or variations and combinations of any of those listed above.

A well-fed cat is not a fat cat; a fat cat is a badly fed cat. Nor is the cat that is properly fed thin; a thin cat may be ravenous. A well-fed cat will eat what is set before it; it is hungry enough never to turn up its nose at wholesome food; it eats as though it enjoyed it. Mealtimes are the big events in a cat's life—mealtimes and the return home of the favorite family member. Both of these events can be made more enjoyable by proper training. There are few things that give the owner more pleasure than to see his pet eat the food he is given with evident enjoyment.

For some reason milk is the first food people think of giving to a cat. Some set a bowl of milk on the floor for the cat to drink instead of water —a great mistake. Milk is in many ways an unnatural food, if a good one. It is no more sensible to say a cat *must* have milk than that an adult human being *must* have it. It is true that cow's milk is much like cat's milk in composition. It is true, too, that the composition of milk acts as a sort of guide for deciding what the relative proportions of protein, carbohydrate, and fat in a diet should be. If this is true, then we should try to compound cat foods to be 85 per cent water, and of the solid materials (the solids in milk being our guide): protein, 27.5 per cent; carbohydrates, 37.2 per cent; fat, 27.5 per cent; ash, 6 per cent—all of which refutes those who tell cat owners not to feed fat. Liquid milk contains about three hundred and twenty calories per pint.

Milk is a fine food. Is it expensive? It costs about ten cents a pound, with three hundred and twenty calories, and 85 per cent is water, but of the remaining 15 per cent, which represents the solids, almost all is digested and absorbed. This is about thirty calories for one cent. Milk is in the category with canned foods, which contain four hundred and fifty calories in each pound and 70 to 75 per cent water, even though the food looks solid. Less of the solids in cat foods are digestible. The better grades cost about fourteen cents per pound (many cans now sold contain fourteen and one half ounces) and therefore give you about thirty calories for one cent.

We must never forget: milk is not water, even though it is fluid. If a cat has milk always before her and drinks a great deal, she needs very little other food. The average cat needs about three hundred and fifty calories a day, the amount contained in one pint of milk and no more. A cupful contains half her nutritional requirements, and many cats drink that much a day.

When you forget that milk is food and give your cat all she wants to drink, you will find it particularly difficult to alter her diet. If you are trying to change in order to get her to eat anything and everything that is good for her, take away the milk too. Don't coax her with special tempting food and don't feel sorry for her. Just offer her a little of the new food, and if she doesn't eat it, very little has been lost. Next day offer her more. She won't refuse it for more than four or five days. By that time she will be hungry enough to eat it, or at least some of it. There is no pain in starvation; the pain is in the owner's mind. It is not unusual for cats to fall in wells, be locked in vacant houses where only water is available, or even be locked out on a roof in a city, and live for thirty or even sixty days without any food whatever. One hates to think of it, yet we must be sensible and honest. There is certainly no cruelty in letting a cat fast long enough to accustom her to eating wholesome food that is good for her.

When a cat refuses food to which she is accustomed, she is either over-fed or sick. Your thermometer can help you to determine whether she has a fever. Her actions may tell you whether she was poisoned; her appetite may tell you by evening she was overfed; a fecal examination can determine if she has worms. She might have a mouth infection, a loose or broken tooth, but in those events she would probably act as if she were going to take a mouthful but stop just short of it. She needs veterinary attention. Here are some practical suggestions you may find useful in feeding your cat:

Warm all the food cats are fed. Cats dislike very cold food.

When you feed, place the food dish on an open newspaper on the floor or on a table. Cats like to drag food out of the bowl. The news-paper can be folded up with the crumbs and thrown away.

Remove any bones which might splinter—poultry and fish bones especially.

It pays to grind the cat's food. Enough for several days may be prepared ahead of time and kept frozen in the refrigerator. Grinding mixes the ingredients well too.

If meal-type foods are used, pour boiling water over them and then mix the additional ingredients.

Cats generally relish some green leafy vegetables well mixed in their food.

If a cat nibbles grass, it may make her vomit, but it does no harm other than sometimes sticking in her throat.

If a cat has a tendency to vomit but is otherwise well, feed her small amounts often.

**Catnip.** The leaves and tops of an herb, *Nepeta cataria*, constitute for a cat one of the most alluring playthings any animal can be given. Cataria was once used medicinally as a drug to reduce gas in the intestinal tract. It is also known as a mild nerve stimulant. In cats it is regarded as some-thing of an aphrodisiac.

When cats eat the leaves they do not digest them nor do they regurgitate them as they do grass, but it is necessary to consume a large amount for the drug to do any damage, and cats seldom eat enough for that.

The odor is what produces the antics, the rolling and playing when catnip is placed where cats can get close to it; they need not eat it at all.

119

# FEEDING

More attention should be paid to the diet of an animal than any other part of its care.

There can be no success if your cat is not properly fed.

It must be clearly understood, if you are starting to breed pedigreed animals, and many of them, they cannot be fed as you would one pet cat, which has its entire liberty and does not breed. Breeding from animals taxes their strength to the utmost, and they must be fed in proportion, or they will become weakly and contract all kinds of diseases, especially skin diseases.

Cats should be fed strictly on a meat diet; no cereals, such at oatmeal, rice, etc.; no potatoes, and, lastly, not a drop of cow's milk, whether it is boiled or not, even should you keep a cow. We had a Jersey cow for some years, but not a cat in the place was allowed milk; in fact, few of them would drink milk after being fed on meat.

Milk feeding causes chronic dysentery, and a cat or kitten so fed is never free from worms. They are also subject to skin trouble, from poverty of blood; in fact, a milk-fed cat is always in a semi-starved condition.

Of course, I know cats have been fed on milk for years, and in many cases they live on it; but the same cat could be changed onto a meat diet with marked improvement.

On the other hand, try changing a meat-fed cat to a milk and cereal diet. The result will be disastrous, the cat soon being reduced to a wreck of its former self.

Meat has been proved by a majority of successful breeders to be the only proper diet for the fancy cat. Raw beef is best, preferably minced, with bones given daily or at frequent intervals, and fresh green grass always accessible.

The quantity given must depend entirely on circumstances. For instance, a cat in the summer months, if not being bred from, needs only two small meat meals a day, or as much as it will eat up quickly. Breeding cats need large meals night and morning, about half a pound of meat each during the day, and in the autumn, about September, let them have all they can eat twice a day, to fatten them up and grow a coat for the winter, giving less about January or February, unless they are kept where it is excessively cold. About March, a pinch of phosphate of soda may be given once a day for a week or two, to cool the blood and prevent the cat shedding its hair too quickly.

Cats "in kitten" should have about six ounces of lean raw meat twice a day, moistened with a little lime-water.

For those keeping a number, I would advise buying a full shin cut of beef or several pounds of neck. Have this cut up and minced; then, in addition to this, a lamb's or sheep's haslet may be cut up and cooked, using only the best parts. Have this minced when cold, and use the gravy to mix it together with the raw meat. A little green vegetable may be added. Always use three parts raw meat to one of any substitute. Never use bread, but dog-cakes broken up and soaked in cold water for twelve hours, then put through the mincer and mixed with three parts raw meat, is also a good diet, as the biscuit is far more nourishing than bread or any other cereal.

Bear in mind that this mixed diet should only be fed to cats which are not breeding, such as neuters, young cats, or old cats which have given up breeding; all kittens, cats "in kitten," or nursing kittens, and all stud cats, should be fed on a pure meat diet.

Fresh lamb or mutton, boned and minced, fed raw, agrees very well with cats. The fat cannot be removed, but when fed raw it does not disagree with them; but lamb or beef should on no account be fed when boiled; lamb becomes too rich, and cooked fat upsets a cat very quickly; the beef becomes hard and indigestible.

Beef hearts and pigs' livers should never be given, and cooked beef liver very seldom; no liver should be fed raw.

I have often wondered how fanciers could write to the cat papers and advocate a mixed cereal and milk diet, with an occasional meat meal. They seem to convince themselves that it is correct, but if you were to see their cats, as I have done, you would notice the poor animals are sorely in want of a good meat diet; and when shown at the winter shows; they are conspicuous for want of coat; they look as if they had forgotten all about winter, and had retained their summer raiment. The fact is, they have only been provided with enough food to keep them alive, and have not had enough nutritious food to grow their coats.

When you observe well-bred, long-haired cats at our winter shows, almost hairless, you can draw your own conclusions; either they have been hopelessly underfed or bred from too often; in some cases both.

It is far more profitable to keep just one or two cats and feed them properly than to keep a number and feed them badly.

Poor diet is the root of most "ills."

# FOOD

Cats should be fed well at regular periods. Bread and milk is an acceptable food to most. Potatoes mixed with meat scraps and gravy may be given now and then; occasionally fish heads, or other fish scraps, boiled with or without rice, are greatly relished. Many cats like porridge in the winter months, and all enjoy getting raw meat off of bones; however, smaller bones of chicken or game should not be given lest they cause internal injury. Cooked meat, in reasonable quantities, should be given each day. Cats are fond of grass, mint and catnip; catnip especially should be harvested in the summer, so that it may be given in the winter. Some advise the feeding of a little raw meat three times a week, but this sometimes produces indigestion, or what is often called "fits." Above all, a dish of clean water should be kept where puss can help herself, for she likes to drink many times a day. Feeding her milk is not compensation for lack of water, therefore her special drinking dish should be kept filled with clean water, where she can reach it at any time.

# COMMON SENSE ABOUT
# CAT FEEDING

C ATS are carnivorous animals. In their wild state they live on hares, rabbits, rats, mice and birds. That is why the perfect diet for domestic cats consists mainly of beef, liver, rabbit, fowl and fish. Nowadays, of course, it is practically impossible to provide your cat with enough of these foods, except fish ; and it is wise therefore to include horse-flesh in the diet. If the meat is really fresh—' fit for human consumption '— it can be given raw, but generally it should be boiled. All offal such as lights (which most cats enjoy) must be boiled.

Fish should always be cooked, and if fish heads are available be sure to boil them well. Always remove all fish bones. Similarly, if you can spare a piece of rabbit or fowl for your cat, remove all bones. There is always the risk of a bone becoming stuck in the throat across the roof of the mouth or even lodged between the teeth ; and if a small bone is swallowed it may pierce the intestines. A large bone, however, may safely be given and it will help to keep your cat's teeth clean and strong. One more word of warning: never give your cat an empty food tin to lick, as his head may get caught in the tin or cut on the sharp edges.

Other foods which should be included in the diet are small quantities of carrots and cooked green vegetables. But while there are certain general principles of cat feeding, there is no hard-and-fast set of rules. Like human beings, cats have varying tastes. Some cats are faddy about certain foods, others will eat almost any suitable food that is put before them. While one cat will not touch sardines, another may eat potatoes or even show a liking for fruit. Common sense, combined with observation of your cat's individual eating habits, is the best guide—in normal times.

Many cats like milk, but it is not a necessary part of their diet after weaning; wild cats never get a drop of milk after they leave their mothers. Needless to say, all cats need water.

If your cat is ill, give him light but nourishing food only. Since food taken willingly has more value than food given forcibly, it is more important to make the 'invalid diet' as tempting as possible. Milk or water should be left within easy reach of the patient except in cases where sickness is present when too much water should not be given.

## HOW MANY MEALS A DAY ?

H E R E again, common sense is the guide. Most grown cats thrive on two meals a day, but mother cats and kittens must, of course, be fed more often (see page 20). Health, age and other factors influence the appetite, and it is impossible therefore to adhere to a strict dietary routine. If your cat leaves half a normal meal uneaten, there is almost certainly something wrong with the food or with the health of the cat. Perhaps he finds the food distasteful, either because he has been given the same food too often or because it is not quite fresh. Perhaps the dish is not quite clean. Perhaps

he is being given too much food, or he is suffering from constipation or some other digestive trouble. Only by careful observation of your own cat will you find the answer. Even in feeding he is an individualist who makes certain demands on your patience and intelligence.

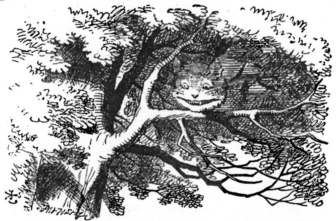

*Sir John Tenniel's famous drawing of the Cheshire Cat in* 'Alice in Wonderland.' *(Reproduced by permission of Macmillan & Co., Ltd., owners of the copyright.)*

## DO CHESHIRE CATS GRIN?

NEEDLESS to say, cats from Cheshire are no more likely to grin than cats from anywhere else. The derivation of the phrase ' to grin like a Cheshire cat ' is not known. It is thought to have originated at a time when Cheshire cheeses were made in the shape of cats which appeared to be grinning. The expression. like many others, was popularised by Lewis Carroll:

' Please would you tell me,' said Alice a little timidly . . .
' why your cat grins like that? '
. ' It's a Cheshire cat,' said the Duchess, ' and that's why.'
— ALICE IN WONDERLAND, *chap. vi.*

RP

Lightning Source UK Ltd.
Milton Keynes UK
UKOW04f0737110214

226258UK00001B/127/P